FIGURES OF THOUGHT

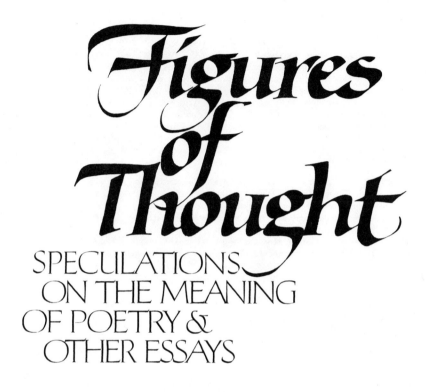

Figures of Thought

SPECULATIONS
ON THE MEANING
OF POETRY &
OTHER ESSAYS

HOWARD NEMEROV

David R. Godine · Publisher · Boston

First edition published in 1978 by
DAVID R. GODINE, Publisher

Copyright © 1978 by Howard Nemerov

ISBN 0-87923-212-9   LCC NO. 77-78361

ACKNOWLEDGMENTS

'Thirteen Ways of Looking at a Skylark' first published in *Poetry;* 'Figures of Thought' in *Sewanee Review;* 'About Time' in *The Structurist;* 'Exceptions and Rules' in *The Bennington Review;* 'On the Resemblances Between Science and Religion' in *The Rarer Action* (Rutgers University Press, 1970); 'Poetry and Meaning' in *Virginia Quarterly Review;* 'The Dream of Dante' in *Prose;* 'Speculation Turning to Itself' and 'On Poetry and Painting, With a Thought of Music' in *Prose* and *The Graduate Journal;* 'Speaking Silence' in *The Georgia Review;* 'The Miraculous Transformations of Maurits Cornelis Escher' in *Artist's Proof;* 'The Winter Addresses of Kenneth Burke' in *Bulletin of College English Teachers of Texas;* 'Thoughts on First Passing the Hundredth Page of *Finnegan's Wake*' in *The American Scholar;* 'Image and Metaphor' and 'What Will Suffice' in *Salmagundi;* 'Poetry and History' in *Virginia Quarterly Review.*

FIRST PRINTING
PRINTED IN THE UNITED STATES OF AMERICA

To Louis D. Rubin, Jr.,
in Friendship & Admiration

CONTENTS

Part One

Thirteen Ways of Looking at a Skylark 3

Figures of Thought 18

About Time 30

Exceptions and Rules 42

On the Resemblances Between Science and Religion 49

Poetry and Meaning 55

The Dream of Dante 71

Part Two

Speculation Turning to Itself 87

On Poetry and Painting, With a Thought of Music 95

Speaking Silence 100

The Miraculous Transformations
 of Maurits Cornelis Escher 115

The Winter Addresses of Kenneth Burke 123

Quidnunc the Poet and Mr. Gigadibs 133

Thoughts on First Passing the Hundredth Page
 of *Finnegans Wake* 138

Part Three

What Was Modern Poetry? Three Lectures 145

 I. *Image and Metaphor* 145

 II. *Poetry and History* 162

 III. *What Will Suffice* 179

Part One

THIRTEEN WAYS
OF LOOKING
AT A SKYLARK

It has been suggested that I discuss what it is like to be a poet these days (the only days in which my opinion could possibly be useful), or, if that is immodest, what it is like to write poetry, what one thinks about the art, what its relation is to the life we supposedly live these days, and so on. This is a fascinatingly large range in which to wander, and I shall be interested to find out what I do think. I hope you will be interested, too. But I must advise you that this will not be a coherently organized essay running in a smooth and logical progression from question to conclusion. Nor will the views expressed necessarily be consistent. I have consulted with my selves, and come up, as usual, with a number of fragmentary notions, many of them aphoristic in expression, and I believe I will do best simply to put these before you without much in the way of explanation or connective tissue.

One thing is immediately brought up by the suggested topic. What is it like to be a poet these days? One thing it is like is this, that you cannot make a living by writing verses, but you can make a quite good living by talking about writing verses. Why is this so? Maybe because, although very few people in America read or buy poetry with any devotion (except while at college) practically everyone in America seems to write poetry, or to have written poetry, at one time in his life. In fact, poetry, like acne, like the development of secondary sexual characteristics, may belong to adolescence—in just this sense, Nietzsche remarked on the close relation between idealism and nubility.

If that is so, the inference is inescapable that a poet is a person who in some sense never got beyond adolescence, or who somehow repeated his adolescence several times during his life. Empirically, there is a good deal of evidence to support that assertion; poets do tend to be a touch Peter Panic. And I have observed, too, that to say even to yourself, 'I have finally grown up, I am a mature human being,' is perilous, it generally means you are about to commit some drastically magnificent folly, such as running away with a sixteen-year-old chick or giving all your savings to an Arthur Murray dance studio or an obscure sect of snake worshippers.

But, observably, that is true not only of poets, but more or less, as a possibility, of everyone. The poet may even have a way of saving himself from the worst excesses of wild delight; he can write a poem. Perhaps it is that we never do really grow up; we go up to the top of the stalk and then revolve, like lollipops. In order to say whether this was good or bad you would have to describe in some detail what being grown up means with respect to the present civilization and your commitment to it: whether, to give the extreme limiting positions, you believed in our way of life unreservedly, or, on the other hand, you were absolutely subversive of everything in it. To see that these two extremes are with us always and have somehow to be dealt with by everyone, it is enough to acknowledge that we live in at least two worlds, one waking, the other dreaming. So to hope for, or try for, the utter eradication of the subversive, in the individual or the nation, would be to hope for or try for the impossible; like the man D. H. Lawrence wrote of who was discontented with the fact that a stick has two ends; he solved his problem by breaking off one of the ends.

You might sum up this part of the thesis by saying that poets are eccentric oddities who on a closer inspection turn out to be eccentric oddities like everyone else. Otherwise put, the poet is the weak criminal whose confession implicates the others.

In any discussion of what it is that poets do, you will not be surprised if you keep coming across that curious phenomenon we have just noticed, of the odd turning into the even.

For example, it is to a first view striking and exceptional that language should be 'poetic' or have a 'poetical' use apart from its ordinary uses of information and command and so on. But a little reflection is enough to show that almost all language, whatever its announced intention, has in addition to its practical purpose a poetical purpose, which is to say a sort of sublime purposelessness demanding attention to itself alone, for nothing else. This is so because poetry, like philosophy, begins in wonder, and the detail-work of this world is both marvelous and mysterious. You can prove this to yourself by taking some perfectly practical piece of language, detaching it by means of a pair of scissors from its context, and letting it dry in the sun for a while; what it loses in information it gains in strangeness:

DOLLAR BILLS GUSH FROM SEWER

That is a headline of some years ago. I don't at all remember, or want to remember, the perfectly rational explanation that no doubt followed. Instead, I am taken with the strikingly unique character of the fact at first, and then, a moment later, by a certain universality behind it. For dollar bills to 'gush' from a sewer is man's deep and ancient dream of Eden, of the land of Cockaigne where precooked chickens fly into your mouth while you yawn. A little further probing reveals something less nice about that dream, for the headline repeats the connection, so well-established in folklore and psychoanalysis, between money and shit, between all man's idealizing symbol systems and his physical reality, as it is asserted in the medieval saying, *Super cloacam ecclesia*.

So that is one way in which the odd turns into the even, the irreducible fact into the universal or general, the unique into the divisible, or meaningful. Another way in which this happens is seen in the chief device of poetry, metaphor, or the assertion of a likeness between different things.

Once I was walking down a road in Austria, a narrow road without a footpath, and was nearly run over by an ambulance racing along on its errand of mercy. At first, again, or anyhow as soon as I had picked myself out of the snow, I was taken with the strikingly unique character of the fact: to be run over by an ambulance was so odd a fate I doubted anyone would believe it nearly happened to me. On the other hand, because of its oddity, I doubted I could have imagined it. But a moment later, the symbolic radiations of the event began to put out their feelers and grasp to themselves more and more of the world, so that it began to seem that 'being run over by an ambulance' was a very fair definition of the paradoxical nature of civilization itself, which comes at you with a gun in one hand and a healing hypodermic in the other.

Not only did the fact thus almost at once spread out into the theory, but the process it seemed to exemplify did too, so that I made the following simple definition of metaphor: metaphor is an exception caught becoming a rule.

One more observation on this anecdote. I said 'a road in Austria,' when for all the difference it makes to the sense of the story I might have said simply 'a road.' Now I suppose one reason for this may have been that I wanted you to believe that I am an extremely sophisticated person, widely-traveled and acquainted with the world; the sort of person who thinks nothing of picking up his suitcase and going off to Austria. (As a matter of fact I am a terrible traveler.) And another reason is that the event I have related did actually happen in Austria, and not in another place. But there may be a third reason, though one not easy to describe. Poetry is characterized by a respect for the fact; that this did happen in Austria makes it appropriate for me to say it did, and the account would feel rather wrong if I laid the scene elsewhere. But in addition, the name of Austria seems (only to me, perhaps) to invest the anecdote with a mystery of uniqueness all its own which is in a degree poetic. The analysis of this circumstance would probably lead us too far away, on too thin and high a wire, to make it serviceable here, but certainly it is related closely to our former assertion that language itself is poetical: for a proper name, more than any other word, introduces into discourse the question of identity, that is, of the uniquely itself and how, in the process of 'coming to mean' something it becomes other than itself. So that a name, in poetry, is always capable of powerful, though very mysterious, effects, as when in Milton Satan lies in the infernal flood,

> *in bulk as huge*
> *As whom the fables name of monstrous size,*
> *Titanian or Earth-born, that warred on Jove,*
> *Briareos or Typhon, whom the den*
> *By ancient Tarsus held . . .*

> (*Paradise Lost,* Book 1, 11.
> 196–200)

Briareos and Typhon are there not simply as examples of giants, to show how big Satan was; they introduce into the poetry the obstinate singularity and irreducibility of tradition and history, which have happened once and do not repeat themselves and so have an immense overplus of being in addition to whatever they possess and yield of meaning. And names in poetry may also show this tradition threatened or overwhelmed:

De Bailhache, Fresca, Mrs Cammel, whirled
Beyond the circuit of the shuddering Bear
In fractured atoms . . .

(T. S. Eliot, 'Gerontion')

To finish off for the moment this inexhaustible theme we should say that poetry works on the very surface of the eye, that thin, unyielding wall of liquid between mind and world, where, somehow, mysteriously, the patterns formed by electrical storms assaulting the retina become things and the thought of things and the names of things and the relations supposed between things. So that in its highest range the theory of poetry would be the theory of the Incarnation, which seeks to explain how the Word became Flesh and why it was necessary for the Word to do this; the explanation which is given to Dante by Beatrice in the Seventh Canto of the *Paradiso* is sublime poetry not least because it is intelligent theory.

Resuming where we have been during the past few minutes, I have tried to show that poetry has to do with the strange interface between fact and meaning, and how this circumstance may be seen in three ways, with respect to the poet himself, with respect to language, with respect to the art of making metaphors. All this began, more or less, with the assertion that poets are people who do not grow up, and the related assertion, which adds the serious reservation that people, too, are people who do not grow up. It is in this sense that I said the poet is the weak criminal whose confession implicates the others, all the others. For as there is nothing new under the sun, so there is no thought so secret or so unique, so wicked or shameful or sublime, that the same has not quietly occurred to many others. Poetry is a realm in which such thoughts, such feelings may be tested without imprecating disaster as a consequence in the practical realm; hence its subversive character is highly civilized and civilizing. Keats says this in a letter: 'What shocks the virtuous philosopher, delights the camelion poet. [Poetry] does no harm from its relish of the dark side of things any more than from its taste for the bright one; because they both end in speculation.' (Keats to Woodhouse, 27 October 1818). So poetry may be thought of as both pedagogic and therapeutic, exploring the whole realm of the possible, and part of the realm of the impossible as well, without settling for one among a million fables as the truth, but also without burning at the stake anyone who happens to disagree.

Another sign of the poet's being a person who does not grow up is his relation, so magical and childlike, with language. His language delights him, it keeps buzzing and humming the world into his ears, and he keeps listening for the word, whether learned or rustic, which by a magical exactitude has grown to belong to what it names in the situation of the moment, for the word of decisive individuality which is paradoxically and for that reason alone a guarantee of meaning: 'All trades, their gear and tackle and trim,' says Hopkins of what is beautiful, and 'All things counter, original, spare, strange.'

But here too the assertion calls forth its opposite. If the poet is childlike, or even childish, in his relation with language, he is also sophisticated and very grown-up in his awareness that his relation with language takes place in language. He says to himself: 'Everything we think we know is a figure of speech,' and 'Every word in the dictionary was beautiful once.' So poets have only rarely been interested in killing people because they say Sibboleth instead of Shibboleth.

Sooner or later someone always says, But what is poetry? The problem there is that I can think of entirely too many answers, which are like excuses in that they lose their effectiveness as their number increases. One would be based on the meaning of the word 'define,' and would say that when people ask you to define poetry they mean 'put a stop to it,' something which definitions have a way of doing. Another would be for me to say: I am trying to be a cloud, so that you can fly at me without hurting yourself. Or you could say, as Augustine said about time, 'I know what it is until I try to tell you' (*Confessions,* Book XI, ch. xiv). Or you could say, somewhat elegantly, that poetry is memory traces mediated by the two words 'I' and 'like' (Christopher Caudwell, *Illusion and Reality* [New York: International Publishers, 1970], p. 208). Or you could say, after Marianne Moore, that the poet presents for inspection 'imaginary gardens with real toads in them' ('Poetry'). A celebrated attempt at definition is given by Archibald MacLeish, in a poem called 'Ars Poetica,' which begins,

> *A poem should be palpable and mute*
> *As a globed fruit*
>
> *Dumb*
> *As old medallions to the thumb,*

and ends by saying that a poem 'should not mean / But be.'

Now it happens that I think this is a beautiful poem, one which speaks eloquently of the endless attempt of the poet to speak the silence. The poet says marvelous things in the less-often-quoted parts of this poem:

> *A poem should be motionless in time*
> *As the moon climbs.*

and gives a beautiful instance of the inexplicable perfection of symbolic speech when he says the poem gives

> *For all the history of grief*
> *An empty doorway and a maple leaf.*

But my admiration for the poem ends rather abruptly when I am asked to consider it as a definition of poetry. Perhaps this happens because the last lines, 'A poem should not mean / But be,' have been so often quoted at me by all sorts and conditions of people who appeared to take some kind of obscure and possibly sinister comfort from them. One answer to the definition offered in those lines would be paradox: the lines do not mean anything, and certainly cannot mean what they say, because they occur in a poem, which should not mean but be. Another answer would be from experience. When I used to help edit a literary magazine called *Furioso,* every mail brought to my desk a large number of poems which perfectly fitted the definition: they meant nothing and there they were.

So one day not long ago I tried to take Mr. MacLeish's famous definition, put it together with Miss Moore's famous definition, which also lends itself to ironic inversion, and wrote these definitions as it were in reverse English, as follows:

A REAL TOAD, WITH IMAGINARY GARDENS IN HIM

> *Nobody had any doubt*
> *From the time his book come out*
> *That these was poems forevermore,*
> *Like the guy wrote the definitions for*

When he said such things as
They was not mean, they was,
Big pear-shaped poems, ready to parse
In the next Creative Writing Clarse.

Yeh, he sure fell flat on his ars
Poetica that time, palpable and mute
As an old globed fruit.

Maybe one way, a negative way, of getting at the definition of poetry would be to say that poetry is a place where contradictions do not destroy one another. For Mr MacLeish's lines remain, to me, as fine as they were before I contradicted them, or gave them a mocking sense. Poetry then would be the place Blake wrote of in *Jerusalem*:

Beneath the bottoms of the Graves, which is Earth's central joint,
There is a place where Contrarieties are equally true:
(To protect from the Giant blows in the sports of the intellect,
Thunder in the midst of kindness, & love that kills its beloved:

(Jerusalem, 48)

In this serious sense, poetry is the sport of the intellect, or what he elsewhere calls 'mental fight,' where everything is possible and desirable because both the bright and the dark, as Keats said, 'end in speculation.' To put this characteristic of poetry into relation with the technique of poetry, seeing that my gibe at Miss Moore's definition and Mr. MacLeish's definition works splendidly without at all destroying the excellence of their phrasing, it will be enough to repeat Isaac Babel's saying about the art of writing: 'A phrase is born into the world both good and bad at the same time. The secret lies in a slight, almost invisible twist. The lever should rest in your hand, getting warm, and you can only turn it once, not twice.'

Maybe you could sum up this part of the discussion by defining poetry as an activity resistant to definition, which certainly remarks something significant about it, or an activity extremely tolerant of definitions, absorbing and transforming these into its own substance just as the Chinese are said to have digested, during many centuries, whole populations of invaders. For there is something rather poetical in a definition, and something rather heroical in the attitude of definition toward the world, if only we are able to realize at the same time, with respect to the subject matter of poetry, that the substance of what is defined does not remain the same.

If so much can be granted, I shall offer a few sentences which do not have the exclusive and inclusive characters of definition, but which may be thought of as first shots bracketing the target and getting the range.

Poetry is like a word containing opposites. If you look for examples of such words, you find that the great central words of philosophical discussion regularly come into the category, e.g., 'reality,' which may mean either what you can see and touch or precisely what you cannot see or touch, and 'form,' which may mean either the inward spirit or the outward shell, and may best be defined as alternatively the inside of an outside or the outside of an inside. We might say that these words were compelled for their survival's sake to evolve in two opposed directions at once, just because they had to accept so very much experience into themselves, and this experience was the experience of contradiction. Poetry is like such words as 'reality' and 'form,' then, because poetry deals first with experience, and only derivatively with meaning; it attempts to catch the first evanescent flickerings of thought across the surface of things. It wants to be as though the things themselves were beginning to speak; they would speak somewhat darkly, the light that came from them would be black light at first.

That may be hard to understand, not only from the somewhat rhapsodic expression I have given it, but also because we do not really at all understand in what way our thought arises out of things, or in what way it penetrates back into things and is capable of making profound changes in their being. If poetry were to be thought of as 'studying' anything, that is what it would be thought of as studying, the opposites and the hope or hopelessness of their ultimate resolution or reconciliation.

For an example, if you contemplate with any candor Shakespeare's *Hamlet,* you realize that you can't say what it means, though you can point to a number of meanings in it. That is because it imitates life, which you might say exhibits at the best a tropism toward meaning, but is not itself a meaning. For a more compassable example, consider one of his greatest sonnets, 'The Expense of Spirit in a Waste of Shame.' This poem lives by the violence of its torment in the face of unbearable and irreconcilable opposites, viewing the tensions of sexuality as pleasurable pain and agonizing pleasure. At the same time, though, it is a triumph of art, perhaps because its formal arrangements take advantage of the very tragedy of its subject matter to set up a sort of alternating current between the extreme poles of the experience, and this alternating current seems to release in us when we read not only the ashamed acknowledgment of our weakness, but also a certain pleasurable notion of our power: reading, it is as though somehow we had rode out a storm and come to some decisive calm.

SONNET 129

Th' expence of Spirit in a waste of shame
Is lust in action, and till action, lust
Is periurd, murdrous, blouddy full of blame,
Sauage, extreame, rude, cruell, not to trust,
Inioyd no sooner but dispised straight,
Past reason hunted, and no sooner had
Past reason hated as a swollowed bayt,
On purpose layd to make the taker mad.
Made In pursut and in possession so,
Had, hauing, and in quest, to haue extreame,
A blisse in proofe and proud and very wo,
Before a ioy proposd behind a dreame,
    All this the world well knowes yet none knowes well,
    To shun the heauen that leads men to this hell.

Looking at the worst, saying how terrible life is—that is what brings out the grand and tragic voice, the voice that speaks 'somewhat above a mortal mouth' (Ben Jonson), the voice that tells us that 'the odds is gone, / And there is nothing left remarkable / Beneath the visiting moon' (Shakespeare).

One way regarded, it is the traditional business of poetry to inspire, even to invent, human purpose. But simultaneously the opposite is true: poetry is the traditional human means of confronting the hopelessness of human purpose. We look, for instance, at the landscape, we look deeply into the landscape which is the quiet background of our lives, we see it waiting there, we know that beautiful as it is it will consume us; and yet there is a relation other than that, benigner than that at least for the time being—for surely it has told us so much about how to be in this world, or how could we have come to know so much, feel so much within us of how to be a tree or a stone or a river? and at certain times, perhaps the darkest times, a twilight at the beginning of the winter, we may feel that not we alone in it, but the landscape itself, *knows* these things; and we may say something like that, with a kind of equivocal humility, our sense for a truth equivocating with despair.

A SPELL BEFORE WINTER

After the red leaf and the gold have gone,
Brought down by the wind, then by hammering rain
Bruised and discolored, when October's flame
Goes blue to guttering in the cusp, this land
Sinks deeper into silence, darker into shade.
There is a knowledge in the look of things,
The old hills hunch before the north wind blows.

Now I can see certain simplicities
In the darkening rust and tarnish of the time,
And say over the certain simplicities,
The running water and the standing stone,
The yellow haze of the willow and the black
Smoke of the elm, the silver, silent light
Where suddenly, readying toward nightfall,
The sumac's candelabrum darkly flames.
And I speak to you now with the land's voice,
It is the cold, wild land that says to you
A knowledge glimmers in the sleep of things:
The old hills hunch before the north wind blows.

Another sentence, as cryptic as the first: Poetry is a species of thought with which nothing else can be done.

I suppose this means a number of quite easy things, though, as well as some more obscure things. Poetry seems to be a unique mode of language in demanding an intransitive attention, an attention to itself, other than and more vital than the transitive attention you give, through it, to what it talks about. One writer on the subject tried to express his sense of this distinction by saying that you read the words of a poem, while with a novel you read through the words to the characters, scenes, and actions represented by the words (Christopher Caudwell, in *Illusion and Reality*).

For instance. In *Measure for Measure* we have Shakespeare's vision of the cold man, Angelo, who has never felt desire until he meets Isabella, whereupon lust overthrows the defenses of an inadequate morality and he becomes villainous, tyrannical, even murderous. The change is radical and sudden, and is reported at first in these lines:

> *The tempter or the tempted, who sins most, ha?*
> *Not she. Nor doth she tempt. But it is I*
> *That, lying by the violet in the sun,*
> *Do as the carrion does, not as the flower,*
> *Corrupt with virtuous season.*

(Act II, Scene 2, 11. 165–168)

The reader of novels, we may say, exaggerating a little as is our privilege, uses these words, and others following them, to perceive, accurately enough, that Angelo is changing in relation to himself as he changes in relation to Isabella, and so on. But that is only the barest abstract of the complex of senses and tonalities reported in the poetry: the violent immediacy of the feeling, for example, that lust is connected with being a dead animal *and* a living flower, that growth and corruption come by the same agency, the only difference being in the response from the inward nature of the patient, that virtue is power as well as goodness, and so related rather to the little violet than to the gross corpse of a beast, that season means a hot taste, a relish, and so has to do with lust, as well as meaning the season of the year, here perhaps spring . . . and a host of other, remoter notions, all radically related to the tight symbolic knot made by the figure of flower, dead beast, and sun.

On the basis of such examples it may be said that poems are in one way like icebergs: only about a third of their bulk appears above the surface of the page.

And another sentence: Poetry perceives the world as a miracle transcending its doctrine, or any doctrine.

Perhaps the plainest sense of that is the circumstance that we are compelled to desire life, even with the clearest view of its end and through so many sufferings on the way; because sorrow is predictable, and even reasonable, while happiness is not, but appears as a momentary unrelated brilliance, like the lightning. It is, one poet says, because life is hopeless and beautiful—giving an equal weight to both words. Poetry speaks of the spirit's being compelled to renew itself, in spite of knowledge, in spite of pain, in spite of death. And it does this by strange means, perhaps inexplicable means. 'The world is charged with the grandeur of God,' Hopkins begins, and that is a mere proposition, except maybe for the one warning word 'charged,' it need not affect us, the line does no more than cock the weapon; in the next, the shot is fired:

It will flame out, like shining from shook foil

('God's Grandeur')

And there it is, utterly convincing. We know it is so, because the saying of it comes spontaneously from the stuff of things, the world has somehow released its charge of the grandeur of God in that irreducible phrase, 'like shining from shook foil.' It is perhaps because, as he says later in that poem, 'There lives the dearest freshness deep down things.' It is the poet's job to look deep down things for that dearest freshness, life's essential oil and incarnate sweetness. And I suppose the poetic faith, about which it is mostly as well to be quiet, includes the corollary tenet to that about looking, that it is not a one-way relation only. For as Hopkins said also, 'What you look hard at seems to look hard at you' (*Notebooks*).

Something too much of this. But there is a poem of Yeats which may do to sum up much of what I have tried to put before you as the attitude of poetry toward the world. It is called 'Lapis Lazuli,' and is about a Chinese relief carved in that stone, a relief which we are to suppose lay before the poet as he wrote. But first, before he comes to that, it is a discussion of what if anything art has to do with this life:

> *I have heard hysterical women say*
> *They are sick of palette and fiddle-bow,*
> *Of poets that are always gay,*
> *For everyone knows or should know*
> *That if nothing drastic is done*
> *Aeroplane and Zeppelin will come out,*
> *Pitch like King Billy bomb-balls in*
> *Until the town lie beaten flat.*

These were probably the same hysterical women who, according to Proust, had Schiaparelli design them austere and uniform-like gowns during the First World War. Against this, the poet sets Shakespeare's images of 'tragic play,' Hamlet and Lear, Ophelia and Cordelia, and says of them that even when they know the end is near, 'The great stage curtain about to drop,' they 'Do not break up their lines to weep,' for 'They know that Hamlet and Lear are gay.'* For life is tragic, and

*Alas! (1975)

the tragic poets have formed its image, and it must be played out: 'It cannot grow by an inch or an ounce.'

In parallel with that vision he now sees another, of 'Old civilizations put to the sword,' of the destruction which all construction evokes, and summons the example of an artist, Callimachus, none of whose works survive. 'All things fall and are built again,' he says conventionally, and adds, less conventionally, that 'those that build them again are gay.'

Now we retire from those apocalyptic scenes and confront the piece of lapis lazuli; the language, which has been energetic sometimes to the point of brutality, becomes quiet. He describes the piece, how it shows two Chinamen followed by a servant carrying a musical instrument, and with a long-legged bird overhead, 'A symbol of longevity.' And then it comes:

> *Every discoloration of the stone,*
> *Every accidental crack or dent,*
> *Seems a water-course or an avalanche,*
> *Or lofty slope where it still snows*
> *Though doubtless plum or cherry-branch*
> *Sweetens the little half-way house*
> *Those Chinamen climb towards, and I*
> *Delight to imagine them seated there . . .*

The sense is so simple, the tone so descriptively calm, that one doesn't at first take it in that this is the heart of the poem, the figure which fuses into harmony all the violence that went before. The art work also has suffered, we are told, the ruining touch of time. And yet it has triumphed, for it has drawn into its imagination, into composition and landscape, hence into the artifice of eternity, everything that time has been able to do to it; every discoloration, crack, or dent, every accident it has suffered in centuries perhaps, has become part of its intention; and it is as though those Chinamen, along with the poet, are aware of this:

> *There, on the mountain and the sky,*
> *On all the tragic scene they stare.*
> *One asks for mournful melodies;*
> *Accomplished fingers begin to play.*

Their eyes mid many wrinkles, their eyes,
Their ancient, glittering eyes, are gay.

One might say of those many wrinkles that perhaps some were put there by the artist, but some came there in the course of time. The nature of things has somehow responded, and a kind of reconciliation has become complete.

And it is possible, drawing on Yeats, to add one more characteristic to our description of poems: we recognize poems because, among other things, 'they do not break up their lines to weep.' They weep, but they do not break up their lines to weep.

FIGURES OF THOUGHT

Thought is the strangest game of all. The players are the Nominalists vs. the Realists. Realists wear colorless jerseys and are numbered One, Many, & All. Nominalists wear crazy quilts instead of uniforms, and their numerals tend to be such things as the square root of minus one. This figure conceals two important circumstances: that there are not in truth Nominalists and Realists, but only the nominalism and realism of each player, who happens to be alone on the field where he plays himself; and that by the tacit pre-game move of dividing into Nominalist and Realist he has made it impossible to win or even finish the game, although—and it is not a little—he has made it possible to play.

Thought proceeds to create the world by dividing it—what? the world, of course—into opposites, as in the initial Yin and Yang of the *Tao Te Ching,* the series of divisions in the first chapter of *Genesis,* the Love and Strife that Yeats took from Empedocles to be the base for the sequent complications of *A Vision,* and so on. Once there are the opposites, a mere two tricks make game. The first is that the opposites will have to bear on one and the other hand the whole weight of the much and many of the world as experienced: every leaf and every star must join one team or the other. The second is that, as a world of opposites is impossible, intolerable, the opposites must be mediated and shown to be one; because, of course, in the world as experienced they *are* one. That was where we began.

A productive model for the enterprise is map-making. Projecting a spherical world on a plane surface involves the cartographer in several distortions for every accuracy, beginning with the creative and mytho-logical decree that there shall be two opposites named East and West; not quite truth, not quite fiction, this prevents any absolute or meta-physical arrivals, or even destinations; on the other hand, it makes—and nor is this a little—navigation possible.

The opposites at first embody themselves in stories. How stories got started is as unknown and like to remain so as how language did (they got together and talked it over among themselves?). With interpretation, whether exegesis or eisegesis, we are in a little better case: Edwin Honig tells us in his lovely book *Dark Conceit,* that the behavior of the gods in Homer and in Hesiod was so scandalous it couldn't possibly mean what it plainly said it meant and had to be allegorized; hence scholiast, who begat rhapsode (like Ion) who begat exegete who begat theologian who begat literary critic who so far has begat nothing but more literary critic; an entire and respectable industry raised upon the strange mythological ordinance that things, in addition to being themselves, hence uninformative enough, had to mean something ... else.

A splendid instance of how all this works except when it doesn't is Lord Bacon's procedure in dealing with the Wisdom of the Ancients. Having first decreed that the figures of Greek myth *meant* something esoteric and wise and opened only to initiates but dark to all the rest of the world, and having then decided, or decreed, that the Sphinx *meant,* of all things, Science, he goes about with equal enthusiasm and ingenuity to translate term for term out of story and into thought, and is able to tell you why Science should have talons, why Science should appropriately be thought of as carried to Thebes on the back of an ass, and so on and so on, not at all indefinitely.

A main consideration to emerge is this: there is a plenty of ways to be wrong in our interpretations, and no way at all to be sure of being right. It is in this respect that the story—the novel, play, poem—is, as Northrop Frye said, silent; and it is in this respect that the story resembles Nature. That is, I may identify a certain tree by as many characteristics as the handbook affords me, but it will never up and say 'You guessed it. I am indeed a box elder.' What we know is never the object, but only our knowledge. Though Milton might well have wanted to condemn Dr. Johnson and approve John Crowe Ransom for what they wrote about *Lycidas,* the poem itself will never do either. What we know is not it, but only our knowledge of it. That may be sad, but it does, as beforesaid, make navigation possible.

How then do we, even tentatively and provisionally, approve one interpretation above another? One possible answer, a humble one concealing, as so often happens, titanic pride: We just like one interpretation better than another, and as soon as we do that we find reasons plentiful as blackberries, just as Lord Bacon did in demonstrating that the Sphinx was, or meant, or represented, Science. We may, and often do, try to recommend ourselves, our interpretations, and the reasons for them to some not quite identifiable community of our fellows, involving ourselves in some risk of tautology, not to mention snobbery—this is the sort of thing you'll like if you're the sort that likes things of this sort, as I do—and an infinite regress, which will probably, however, be put a stop to by a change in Fashion, that last and most pervasive and secret of mythologies.

Harold Bloom's *The Anxiety of Influence* (New York: Oxford University Press, 1973) is offered as A Theory of Poetry. It is praised by no less sufficient an authority than Morris Dickstein, as 'The most provocative and original piece of literary theory in English since Frye's *Anatomy of Criticism.*' I can agree to provocative; I was provoked. And to original as well, but only in the sense of Dr. Johnson's saying that when the cow ran dry you could always milk the bull. But my trouble with the book may merely have been that it was too difficult for me, as I am afraid my brief description of its contents must inevitably show.

Bloom begins with the beguiling simplicity—but it is the last one we are to meet—of his premise: poets are influenced by the poets who have gone before them. His figurative way of describing the situation also looks simple at first: the problems of poets in dealing with the influence of past poets, or with the anxiety attendant upon it, are comparable with the problems people have in growing up, or dealing with the influence of the parents (though to Bloom the Father alone seems important), so that the model in both instances is what Freud called, 'with grandly desperate wit,' the family romance. Upon this base the author quickly erects a large rhapsodic apparatus of specialized terms and perhaps somewhat too many characters.

The ways in which the new poet (ephebe) copes with the old poet (precursor) are six in number, and their names are: Clinamen, Tessera, Kenosis, Daemonization, Askesis, and Apophrades. These Six Revisionary Ratios, as Bloom calls them, are summarized in an Introduction. One example will be fair to give, and as it must stand for all I rolled a die and came up with:

> 5. *Askesis,* or a movement of self-purgation which intends the
> attainment of a state of solitude; I take the term, general as it is,
> particularly from the practice of pre-Socratic shamans like Em-

pedocles. The later poet does not, as in *Kenosis,* undergo a revisionary movement of emptying, but of curtailing; he yields up part of his own human and imaginative endowment, so as to separate himself from others, including the precursor, and he does this in his poem by so stationing it in regard to the parent-poem as to make that poem undergo an *askesis* too; the precursor's endowment is also truncated.

(*The Anxiety of Influence,* introduction)

Rating the above for difficulty, I should say it is harder than Clinamen, much easier than Apophrades, and about the same as the other three.

These titles head up the six main chapters, to which are added a Prologue, an Interchapter called A Manifesto for Antithetical Criticism, and an Epilogue. Prologue and Epilogue are about the Fullness, the Father, the Path, and sound enough like a statement of faith that I may excuse myself from dealing with them; the Manifesto, however, is criticism, and I cite a few provocative and original sayings from it:

> Every poem is a misinterpretation of a parent poem.
> There are no interpretations, but only misinterpretations, and so all criticism is prose poetry.
> The best critics of our time remain Empson and Wilson Knight, for they have misinterpreted more antithetically than all others.
> Criticism is the discourse of the deep tautology . . . . the art of knowing the hidden roads that go from poem to poem.

Alas, I do not know whether these things are so or no. If I too admire Empson and Wilson Knight I have evidently been doing so for thirty years for the wrong reasons. Bloom is unflinching about accepting the consequences of his axioms: he really does believe that his book is a poem, 'A theory of poetry that presents itself as a severe poem . . .' It doesn't *look* like a poem. And it doesn't *sound* like a poem. But if he says it's a poem? He ought to know, he wrote it, didn't he?

While he limits himself to assertion, Bloom is on privileged ground. But the two brief appearances of reasoned argument in what I have quoted—'and so' in the second sentence and 'for' in the third—don't at all appear to me to connect, and I am tempted to think of Bloom that his form is logic but his essence is confusion. Nor is it at all easy to improve one's opinion as to whether these things are so or no by applying to the six main chapters, for Bloom's explanations routinely

seem to make things worse, as in, e.g., a paragraph about 'Binswange-
rian *Versteigenheit* (or 'Extravagance,' as Jacob Needleman wittily trans-
lates it),' about which my bewilderment is not resolved by being told
that 'Binswanger's summary is useful if we read it backwards.' Maybe
my problems with Bloom's thoughts are problems merely of style; but
what's so mere about that?

One minor nuisance. Bloom improves his quotations from the masters by adding their intentions, tones of voice, and even probable facial
expressions, as in 'Freud, with grandly desperate wit,' above, and
'Kierkegaard . . . announces, with magnificently but absurdly apocalyptic confidence . . .' And he can go further along this line, not only
reading Binswanger backwards but telling us what Nietzsche might
have thought had he lived to read Freud. But there are greater difficulties than that.

Bloom writes a literary and allusive shorthand which is, moreover,
almost entirely associative; one thing reminds him of another and he
can't stop, so that he is sometimes nothing but ellipsis, all beads and
no string. On a single page he names, not merely in a catalogue but in
what is proposed as a series of related relations, Goethe, Nietzsche,
Mann, Emerson, Thoreau, Blake, Lawrence, Pascal, Rousseau, Hugo,
Montaigne, Johnson, Aristotle, Homer, Arnold, Keats, Kierkegaard,
several of them more than once. Not counting the repetitions, this
amounts to one name every two lines, and is very hard to understand.
No doubt that to the formidably learned author each use of each of
these names stands for something he could identify far more precisely;
but to the reader the game becomes merely bewildering in a short
while. Finally I thought to recognize the source of this idiom as the
graduate seminar; just to have done the required reading is not enough,
you have to have done it in the last twenty minutes.

Bloom has too many hypostases, too many nonce characters, more
terms than he has work for them to do. The principal ones are the Six
Revisionary Ratios, which are held to be *the* six ways in which poets
may handle—or fail to—the anxiety of influence. After being summar-
ily described, these terms are treated throughout as unquestionably
distinct clinical entities, as real as if each one had been abstracted from
hundreds or thousands of cases, when in fact the whole field of observation contains not many more than half a dozen major instances from
Milton on, and maybe a dozen more fleetingly alluded to.

In addition to the six principal terms and the anxiety of influence
itself there are ephebe and precursor (he doesn't always capitalize his

characters), The Covering Cherub (by Blake out of Genesis and Ezekiel), The Idiot Questioner (Blake, in *Milton*), a bald gnome called Error and his two little cousins, Swerve and Completion (the feeling of having strayed into a comic book grows stronger here), and as many more as you can or care to identify by the mode of their generation and decay, of which the following gives an instance:

> Chomsky remarks that when one speaks a language, one knows a great deal that was never learned. The effort of criticism is to teach a language, for what is never learned but comes as the gift of a language is a poetry already written—an insight I derive from Shelley's remark that every language is the relic of an abandoned cyclic poem. I mean that criticism teaches not a language of criticism (a formalist view still held in common by archetypalists, structuralists, and phenomenologists) but a language in which poetry is already written, the language of influence, of the dialectic that governs the relations between poets *as poets*. The poet *in every reader* does not experience the same disjunction from what he reads that the critic in every reader necessarily feels. What gives pleasure to the critic in a reader may give anxiety to the poet in him, an anxiety we have learned, as readers, to neglect, to our own loss and peril. This anxiety, this mode of melancholy, is the anxiety of influence, the dark and daemonic ground upon which we now enter. (p. 25; italics in original)

Chomsky's remark *is* an illuminating one; indeed, it is a key to his work. But what save rhapsodic association governs its relation with the ensuing sentences? Unless Bloom has some other source of Shelley's remark than the celebrated place in the *Defence,* the remark is really quite different: 'Every original language near to its source is in itself the chaos of a cyclic poem.' I don't know that the difference makes much difference to the argument, for I'm not at all certain what the argument is, though Bloom's misremembering suits his theme of melancholy declension, influence, and anxiety, better than Shelley's Romantic fervor about origin and source. Further, I am aware that there are these three ways of reading, as reader, as poet, as critic. But the hypostasis of them as three distinct persons together with the permutations mentioned—and those not mentioned but which the reader trying to negotiate the sentence to its end may already be fearfully anticipating—makes hash of what sense may be intended.

If you took the key sentence beginning with what he means ('I mean . . .') and removed that parenthesis during which you spent three weeks in the stacks, you would still not be quite out of the woods:

> I mean that criticism teaches not a language of criticism . . . . but a language in which poetry is already written, the language of influence . . . (p. 25)

Reader, this statement is made by the same fellow who has just handed out his half-dozen Revisionist Ratios, Kenosis. . . . Apophrades, holding them to be the nub of the matter, and now declares that criticism does not teach a language of criticism. My ho head halls. What criticism teaches, he says, is a language in which poetry is already written, e.g., finding the Emerson in Stevens, the Milton in practically everyone? No doubt this is a rich territory for scholarship; but criticism? When I dreamed long ago about an art critic who went to the museum to measure the distance between paintings I thought it was hyperbole, but now it turns out to be Bloom.

He does admit at least once to a doubt about the enterprise, ascribing it to his own Idiot Questioner: 'What is the use of such a principle, whether the argument it informs be true or not?'

> Is it useful to be told that poets are not common readers, and particularly are not critics, in the true sense of critics, common readers raised to the highest power? And what *is* Poetic Influence anyway? Can the study of it really be anything more than the wearisome industry of source-hunting, of allusion-counting . . . .?
> (p. 31)

And he develops the doubt for another ten lines citing Eliot, Emerson, Frye, and Arnold. But he overcomes it.

Such doubts as may occur to a reader, however, or as did occur to a poet, Wallace Stevens, get the usual short Freudian shrift. There are two devices which may be appropriate to the analytic session, as from doctor to patient, but which, when used in discourse between supposed equals, turn brutal and vulgar. One is to say that if the reader is not conscious of the problem then he must be *unconscious* of it. Bloom's example is Stevens. The other is to say that if the reader thinks an idea inapplicable, inaccurate, or plain not true, he has a *resistance* to it. Bloom's example is Stevens. And the final flip is to say that one's denial is an example of what one is denying; thus Bloom, after quoting

Stevens (including 'I am not conscious of having been influenced by anybody'):

> This view, that poetic influence scarcely exists, except in furiously active pedants, is itself an illustration of one way in which poetic influence is a variety of melancholy or anxiety-principle. (p. 7)

As for the Six Revisionary Ratios themselves, I cannot tell the reader whether they are so or no, whether they exist or not. Kenneth Burke once quoted C. S. Peirce on the usefulness of 'words so unattractive that loose thinkers are not tempted to use them,' with this sequel:

> It is vital for science that he who introduces a new conception should be held to have a *duty* imposed upon him to invent a sufficiently disagreeable series of words to express it.
>
> (*Attitudes Toward History* [New York: *The New Republic,* 1937] Vol. I, p. 10)

Peirce called this 'the moral aspect of terminology,' and surely Bloom has done his moral duty. But though the terms are sufficiently disagreeable, are they science? These ways of being influenced, or of showing it, exist only for so long as enough of us agree with Bloom that they do; built into the nature of things they are not. Even in science, alas, if the new conception you introduced happened to be phlogiston or dormitive virtue or the luminiferous ether, you would no doubt do well to distinguish a half-dozen varieties of each by wonderful names.

I've a good few more quarrels with Bloom, both style and substance. But sufficient unto the day. I guess the main one is that though I agree to influence as a fact, and agree that the project of Coriolanus ('as if a man were author of himself and knew no other kin') is unlikely to work for any of us, I hold to the belief that you do at last grow up and stand there on your own, as what Philip Rieff called 'the healthy hypochondriac who rightly expects to survive all interpretation' (*The Triumph of the Therapeutic* [New York, 1966], p. 40). When you begin, you write: 'The grass is green,' and everyone says 'Aha! Wallace Stevens.' Twenty years later you write: 'The grass is green,' and it sounds just like you. This is a mystery, with which relation durst never meddle.

But Bloom, as far as I make him out, doesn't believe it. Even his 'strong poets' (he's very high on poets being *strong*), the ones whose poems 'most move me'—the only statement made independently of apparatus that I found in the whole book, a touching moment indeed—, even those poets, A. R. Ammons and John Ashbery, are much diminished in comparison of the former times:

> *And as in lasting, so in length is man*
> *Contracted to an inch, who was a span . . .*

> (John Donne, *The First Anniversary*)

The world just is degenerate from Milton's day, that's all. The myth latent in Bloom's book is perhaps the oldest one of all, an inheritance already aeons old in the Hindu tradition when the anxiety of its influence affected Daniel and Hesiod, Ovid, Dante, Peacock . . . and Bloom. It is the Myth of the Four Ages, of which the first three range from paradisal to endurable but happen to be mythological, while the fourth miserable one is perfectly real and happens to be home to us. Bloom doesn't appear to notice this, but he states the sequence plainly enough. Shakespeare is out of it; he 'belongs to the giant age before the flood' (and Marlowe his precursor just wasn't big enough to matter). So the four ages are: Milton, the Enlightenment, Romanticism, and 'a further decline in its Modernist and post-Modernist heirs.'

From Bloom's book I derive three melancholy lessons, or laws.

1. That the life of the institutionalized intelligence, as by its own sort of entropy, grows ever more difficult and never less so.

2. That intelligence itself, which is responsible for so much of the small freedom we have or can use, is intrinsically committed to determinism. That is one way of expressing the curse on knowledge.

3. That the effort to render English unintelligible is proceeding vigorously at the highest levels of learning.

It is the more reassuring, then, to have Denis Donoghue's *Thieves of Fire* (New York: Oxford University Press, 1973) as a moving demonstration that none of the three is necessarily true.

There are a few ways in which the two books are alike, and the comparison is illuminating as to the differences as well. Both are short, both are about interpretation, the principle of action in both is the application of a myth to several writers, Milton being the one they have in common and the one they begin with in principle as well as in time. Beyond this, though, they resemble one another mainly as opposites might be thought to do; in the terms of Pascal's famous antithesis Bloom is geometry and Donoghue is finesse.

Donoghue's myth is that of Prometheus, and because his book began as the T. S. Eliot Memorial Lectures for 1972 at the University of Kent the author must have faced a pretty problem in manners right at the start, for not only was Eliot himself the least Promethean of poets, he also had the most serious and grave reservations, however now and again qualified, about all Donoghue's Private Prometheans: Milton, Blake, Melville, Lawrence. I am glad to say Donoghue's solution is as elegantly courteous as his problem may have been shrewd, as time after time Eliot is brought in to have his say from the shades, reminding the author and his readers that the Promethean is not the only kind of literature, and certainly not the only one worth having.

Thieves of Fire seems to me a beautiful example of thought at its work of creating by dividing; of the use of myth as an instrument or figure of thought: 'The myth of Prometheus begins as a story, an anecdote of transgression, but because many generations have found it significant it has become a category, one of the available forms of feeling' (p. 18). In Donoghue's deep and sensitive reading, the story of the theft of fire, with the associated stories of cheating Zeus out of the sacrifice and of Epimetheus and Pandora, becomes the story of the Fall which is also the Rise: the fire is not only what broils the flesh and forges the sword, it is also thought, consciousness, conscience, guilt; our first benefactor being also the first great thief, and we ourselves uneasy with the gift because we are connivers and receivers of stolen goods. 'Prometheus provided men with consciousness as the transformational grammar of experience' (p. 26).

From the story, too, comes the figure and character of Prometheus as an identifiable type of mind, or imagination:

> There is no evidence that Zeus thought any the better of men for
> their new skills. The imagination has always been a contentious
> power, as a result, so far as men are concerned in their relations
> with the gods. A typology of the imagination would be an expli-
> cation of the several ways in which men have risen above them-
> selves by the possession of consciousness. The Promethean imagi-
> nation is only the most extreme gesture in that account, and it is

not alone in featuring arbitrary defiance in men, a show of force in the gods answered by a show of blasphemy in men. The predicament remains: imagination, the divine power in men, falsely acquired, stolen from the gods in the first of many similar outrages. Since then, the Promethean imagination has always been defiant: it starts with an incorrigible sense of its own power, and seeks in nature only the means of its fulfilment. (pp. 26–27)

Thought of this kind delights me by its clarity and serviceableness; and an integral part of the delight is Donoghue's modesty, tact, and sense of limits: simplification is a necessity of thought, but all simplification is oversimplification: 'There is no thought which embraces all our thought,' he says, quoting Merleau-Ponty and going on to his own equally engaging formula for the tragedy of mind: 'One of the deficiencies of anything is that it is not also something else.'

Out of this balanced good sense emerges not only the Promethean imagination with its titanic powers and devastations, its sense of destiny's being, as Rilke said, *always against,* but its antitype, the imagination receptive and obedient; 'content with ready procedures and with the range of feeling which they allow . . . . he hands his feeling over to the language, and is happy to abide by its determination.' That is said in description of Herbert's 'Decay' as over against Milton's sonnet 'On the Late Massacre in Piedmont,' and a similar balance obtains between Wordsworth and Blake.

Donoghue is especially convincing about the consistency of his related relations as to their characterizing presence in attitudes to language, nature, and God or the gods: his poets are compared as 'prescriptive' or 'descriptive,' as modelers imposing their own thought upon the material and even upon its recalcitrance, or as carvers concerned to release from the material significance felt to be already present in it.

The feeling I got over and over from *Thieves of Fire* is that its author is making his cuts through reality just at the joints, and that is why it looks so easy. I am sadly conscious of having given much more time to saying why I don't like Harold Bloom's book than I am able to give to saying why I do like Denis Donoghue's book; a matter of the squeaky axle getting the grease. And I suppose it may be said that my likes and dislikes are, after all, arbitrary. But I would add one criterion for 'liking' that may be thought to relieve it at least somewhat of its absolute subjectivity, willfulness, or capriciousness, though it too must, I suppose, depend ultimately on my feeling that it is so. That criterion is the production of insight, the power conferred on the author by his metaphor, or myth, of producing one after another observation about literary works and about the imagination that impress his reader as fresh, useful, true (remembering always that interpretation *is* misinterpretation, or, as Augustine put it, 'What I am telling you is true in a way *because* it is false in a way.') I think Donoghue has had great and merited good luck in this respect; time after time I find him making remarks, whether he is interpreting the story of Prometheus itself or using it to illuminate certain traits in his authors and their books, that arouse my warmest admiration—together with, of course, that bare edge of envy that alone guarantees my feeling that he is getting things right: 'Yes, of course, why couldn't I have thought of that myself?' Donoghue's interpretations, in detail as in the large, bring conviction because they illuminate. I can't bring the two sides of criticism's tautological equation any closer together than that, and had best stop right there.

ABOUT TIME

When men first began to name their experience, how ever in the world could they have gone about it? And what a tricky question that is, which however you put it down invites you to answer its prior question: How shall I rightly be asked?

For it is hard if not impossible to ask this sort of question without sneaking the answer into the terms of the asking. 'First,' 'began,' 'Name,' are all ways of smuggling the answer, or an answer, into the question, hence of preventing inquiry before it can get off the ground. For by assuming a time at which men 'began' to name their experience, I have assumed already the existence of the medium in which they did so, their language. And since I want to ask concerning the names men found for time and its action, I have to observe that languages, with their ingenious spread of tenses, are already and without further application descriptive of beliefs about time. All the same, I like to think it took a very great poet to invent such expressions as 'time passes,' 'the passage of time,' 'time past.'

For like a good many things in this world that look to be obvious, this one is not so obvious at all when looked at closely. That time passes is an item of my belief as of yours; it is scarcely ever questioned by anyone except lovers, shamans, priests, poets, and physicists, and by these only on certain occasions and in specific applications. But for all men on almost all of their errands in the world it is accepted that time passes; it simply does.

And yet 'time passes' is a metaphor, a piece of poesy. Like the other mightiest powers—God, death, money are examples—time has a secret name which it forbids us to use, and so it may be spoken of only in metaphors.

For instance. One of the most commonly accepted ways of thinking about time is to think about a road. For Proust the project of seeking for the past takes this topographical form, it is 'suivre au clair de lune ces chemins ou je jouais jadis au soleil,' to retrace by moonlight the roads where I used to play in the sun. What a beautiful and spiritual figure that is, in which experience is under the aegis of sunlight and memory is its pale replication, with all the color leached away. Yet all the same it is a figure, that is to say a compound of likeness and unlikeness, productive of tensions. Time is a road because the course of life is like a journey in which one place after another is left behind. But what a strange sort of road it is, on which if you turn around and go back the way you came you will still be going in the same direction! And which of us has taken off at right angles to the road of time in order to picnic in a field beside it? And where is it going, this road of time? From the past into the future, or from the future into the past? Even the idea that a road 'goes' is a metaphor; really the road lies there, and it is we who go. And yet some lasting intuition of the common speech says that the road 'goes' through the mountains, and when we travel it is the road that 'gets us there.'

Maybe metaphor must be carried to the point of contradiction, of self-contradiction, if the figure of the road is to deal successfully with more than one of the phenomena associated with time. In Edwin Muir's strange and wonderful poem 'The Road' (*Collected Poems* [New York: Oxford University Press, 1965]) this happens.

> *There is a road that turning always*
> *Cuts off the country of Again.*
> *Archers stand there on every side*
> *And as it runs time's deer is slain,*
> *And lies where it has lain.*

In that country of Again odd things happen and do not happen, all at the same time:

> *There the beginning finds the end*
> *Before beginning ever can be,*
> *And the great runner never leaves*
> *The starting and the finishing tree,*
> *The budding and the fading tree.*

And the poet's clinching instance, at the end of this poem, is the future as it lies blind and folded in the seed, the future conceived as an endlessly repeated Fall of Man.

If time may be spoken of only in metaphors, there is a corollary to
that as well: everything in the world is metaphorical of time; whatever
else it expresses, it expresses an aspect of time as well. At the tempo of
the mountain or the tempo of the candle flame, from the melting of
glaciers to the rapid metabolism of the hummingbird, the world is
telling of time, telling the time, helplessly singing the song of coming
and going and staying; of staying-in-going and going-in-staying,
which is most visibly the music scored for the mountain stream, so that
we also commonly say that time is a stream; for Yeats it is a stream that
has its source at both ends:

> *All the stream that's roaring by*
> *Came out of a needle's eye;*
> *Things unborn, things that are gone,*
> *From needle's eye still goad it on.*

> (*Collected Poems* [New York:
> Macmillan, 1956])

The eye cannot rest on running water; and neither can the mind in
time: there is no now. Or else the now is not in time at all, and as a line
is said to be made up of dimensionless points time is made up of
timeless instants, every one of which must somehow be in eternity.
Ananda Coomaraswamy (*Time and Eternity* [Ascona, Switzerland: Ar-
tibus Asiae, Supplementum 8, 1947]) has this parable in illustration:
when you throw a ball straight up in the air, the instant at which it
stops before coming down is *now*. But really the ball does not stop, for
throwing a ball straight up is but the limiting case of throwing the ball
into any trajectory whatever, hence rise and fall are continuous with
one another. And that moment at which the ball did *not* stop at the top
of its rise—that moment which does not exist—is *now*. Which led
another poet to a moment of revelation: 'I see,' he said, 'that now is a
razor made of glue!' As a friend of his had remarked, 'A metaphor may
be all the better for being absurd.'

The problem, and is it merely—merely!—a linguistic one? I spoke
earlier of the common metaphor that speaks of time as a road, and
remarked it was a strange road indeed on which if you turned around to
retrace your steps you would still be going in the same direction. But
the unconscious wisdom of metaphor may be as great as its equally
unconscious errors; for this is exactly—no, inexactly, and yet

significantly—what happens with respect to time, that medium (if it is a medium) wherein I go into the future at every instant in just the degree that I go into the past at every instant. This holds true of me, and also of everyone and everything about me. I must try to see this strange situation more clearly.

From where I sit writing away at this, I have a view of various motions and stillnesses. Raindrops are falling from the eaves, melting the icy snow on the bird feeder whereto now and again a chickadee or jay comes flying in to feed. Now and again, too, a car drifts through the few yards of the street open to my view. Here inside the room there is the usual furniture standing with its usual stolidity and air of permanence.

But all this, the chair as much as the raindrop, whether moving or standing, is at every instant moving into the future and moving into the past simultaneously. I am an instant older, and no doubt different, if imperceptibly so, from the I who was an instant younger an instant ago, and who is now irrecoverable. The desk is an instant further along on its progress from seed to tree to artefact to dust.

Now the raindrop changes both its position and its condition a great deal faster than the desk does. But that is only with respect to visible space; with respect to time, both raindrop and desk are moving into the past and the future at exactly the same rate, and so am I.

My question, then, is this: If I and everything open to my observation are moving through time at the same rate of time, how do I know it? I do not mean to doubt the common wisdom of the world on this theme, which from time immemorial has observed correctly that living things always grow older and never grow younger; whence many consequences proceed, among them the Second Law of Thermodynamics; I mean only, but rather strictly, to ask how I know that it is so.

I do not think this question can be easily resolved by the usual reference to the motions of heavenly bodies, the change of seasons, alternation of day and night, pulse, hunger, and so on, for these are observations of change, and they enable me to perceive only that as I am compelled to speak figuratively when I speak of time, the figures I am compelled to use must be drawn from the realm of space and movement in space, where alone I find visible analogues for what I suppose happens in time, or for what I suppose time does. Even to say something as simple and obvious as 'I am moving through time' or 'Time is moving through me' is metaphorical.

What I am looking for, in this subject as in any, is the poetic quality of *strangeness;* which I might define as whatever the marvelous power of language causes to remain hidden from us in the simplest sayings. And the strangest thing my observations have so far produced must surely be this: that as we habitually draw our notions of time from movement in space, there remains in hiding the idea that whatever is in time is traveling simultaneously in two directions at once, into the future and into the past, and at exactly the same rate.

This is terribly hard to think about; in fact it seems to forbid thought. How odd it is, and how unsatisfactory, to have to say: In the five minutes it took to write the last paragraph I—or x, or everything in the universe—traveled five minutes into the future, but only because the same—or another?—I or x or everything traveled five minutes into the past. I make no doubt that I grew older without growing younger during the five minutes; yet it remains as obvious as it is inexplicable that whatever goes into the future goes into the past by the same amount.

What in the world shall I do with this thought? Take five years off and study physics? or the physiology of the brain? Read St. Augustine again? He said of time, as I remember, 'I know what it is until I try to tell you' (*Confessions,* XI, xiv).

Perhaps I should be told, probably by a linguistic analyst, 'This is purely and simply a linguistic hang-up; stop it, drop it, you not only are getting nowhere but you are never going to get anywhere. Or rather, now you've seen the dilemma exists as a result of the existence of language itself, go have a drink and forget about it.'

That's a tempting idea, linguistic analyst. And I might yield to the temptation, if I didn't suddenly see that you are doing what you customarily do, putting down great and unquestionable realities as mere linguistic fictions only because, being invisible, they are a little hard to see. Outside of a school of philosophy, no one—not I, certainly—doubts the real existence of past and future, or of a somewhat, a process, an ongoing, which we call *time,* and which, whether we call it so rightly or wrongly, affects everything. No, what I am trying to see is what happens when we call in question our metaphorical presuppositions about its nature and its action; and the first thing I have seen, which is admittedly most baffling, is that things move into the future and the past at one and the same time.

A metaphor about time, then, will have to satisfy two seemingly incompatible requirements: First, that everything gets older, not younger; second, that in the course of doing this irreversible thing, everything goes into both past and future at once.

But I see that there remains in my way of putting the matter some contamination from the realm of space. Growing older, that's all right; but 'going' and 'going into' are deceitful; they will have to go, for they make trouble by suggesting that past and future are places, if not actually boxes of some kind; and to make my first requirement symmetrical with my second, I should have to say what is not true, that things get older and younger at once, or else how could they *go into* the future, where they are older, and the past, where they are younger?

Suppose a rope. Suppose it to be under tension and to be slowly and steadily moving in one direction, say from left to right. I am a fiber in the rope, one of many such, and my spiral existence is bounded by two points, B and C, along the length of the rope. At a point A on the left I did not exist, and at a point D on the right I shall exist no more. I know—somehow—that I am moving, along with the many other fibers that make up the rope, into the future; perhaps the other fibers have always told me so, and that is how I am able to say that I know it; for when I inspect my experience as a fiber, it turns out to be an experience of tension; and of course you cannot have an experience of tension from one end alone, but you have to experience it as equal at both ends. In some sense, I am being pulled equally by past and by future, and it is not possible for me, as a fiber, to know which is which.

Reasoning by analogy is said to be dangerous, though I wonder if there is any other way of reasoning that will do to initiate thought at all. In any event, the advantage of analogy is that one can inspect it afterward, take as much or as little as seems to apply to the matter analogized, and move on. So in my figure of the rope and its fibers, though it is a figure derived from space, or existing in space, like the others we have mentioned, we do get somewhere; not everywhere, but not nowhere either. For the figure does satisfy the more neglected requirement of a metaphor dealing with time by bringing in tension and the fact, evident in experience, that tension cannot be experienced at one end alone but has to be experienced as double and opposite. If the fiber does not know from its own feelings that it, along with the other fibers that compose the rope, is moving steadily in the direction AD, well, I do not know from my own feelings at this moment that I and all about me are moving steadily in the direction called future—in order to do which, I say again, I and all about me have to be moving steadily in the direction called past equally and at an equal rate, a condition which my figure fails to satisfy.

Maybe the trouble is with nouns. Could it be that the I moving into the future is not the same as the I moving into the past? that we have something like a pair of mirrors reflecting one another (Augustine's image for Despair) while moving steadily away from one another? or are the pair of us in some strange way the same and not the same? In the light, or the darkness, of this consideration it seems appropriate to look back more closely at my own experience.

I am growing older. But this is not something I derive from the immediate experience of this now, this present, this hour, this day. If it is a truth that I derive from experience at all it must be drawn from a much greater mass of experience than my present feelings. But this greater mass includes much experience that is not immediately my own but has been told me and exemplified to me by other people, in books, and so on. I know, for instance, that I live in a society more dynamic and more time-oriented than any other in the history of the world, a society whose emblem of servitude might well be the watch, with its strap or chain or shackle. This is a fairly recent development, too; only a few centuries ago, when second hands were introduced, Mme. de Sevigne wrote that she wouldn't wear a watch that chopped up time so fine; and since then we have arrived at microseconds. Perhaps if I lived in a less 'progressive' medium of civilization, in some quiet backwater as they say, my experience of time (with my notion of tension in it) would be incalculably different. And even within my society there exist many different class and occupational differences with respect to the sensing of time; where one sees it as a road leading onward, another as an urgently and relentlessly pouring stream, a third might experience time as a still pool or a broad meadow in sunshine. Probably, indeed, the collective time we read from clocks, the one that is theoretically the same for everyone and moving at a constant speed from the beginning of the universe to the end of the universe, is an entity as fictitious as money, and as mysteriously powerful. Which reminds me of the key proverb of our society, said to have been invented by Benjamin Franklin: Time is Money.

There is a plain practical sense, or even two plain practical senses, in which that saying is easily understood by everyone. Probably the intention is prudential: if you use your time rightly, i.e., *profitably,* you will make money; whereas if you *waste* the time you will remain poor. And the second such literal or practical sense is the one you learn when you take a mortgage on your house. But as the object of this meditation is to find the strange and ordinarily hidden poetical quality in commonplace sayings, I am compelled to look further into the connections between time and money. (On occasions of this sort I do wish I knew more, but the plain fact is that I don't).

I remember that Rilke, in the *Notebooks of Malte Laurids Brigge,* has a beautiful, funny, sad fable about a man named Nikolai Kuzmich. I'm sorry I don't have it handy to quote entire, but the sense of it is that Nikolai Kuzmich one day realized that time was money and began to congratulate himself on being so rich. Presently, however, he had doubts. Perhaps he should save some of his enormous store, and not keep changing it into the small change of minutes and hours that vanished so readily and so alarmingly? But try as he would to save an hour here and an hour there, it always happened at the end of the week that he had spent the same time as he had the week before. The upshot of it was that poor Nikolai Kuzmich began to remember how they used to say in school—though they slid by it rather glibly—that the earth was in motion around the sun . . . and upon the close consideration of that, he went to bed and never got up again.

Time is Money. Try to think that thought right through.

Time is said to be established by the movements of the heavenly bodies in space. I am in no position to doubt it, but it has often seemed to me a trifle odd and capricious that whatever is represented by the endless revolvings of earth around sun and moon around earth, so calm as these appear, should be capable of such catastrophic, though doubtless trivial, effects as my birth, my life, my death.

But the coinage of gold and silver into discs also relates to the same heavenly bodies and even to their relations. Norman O. Brown, following Keynes, says this:

> The special attraction of gold and silver is not due to any of the rationalistic considerations generally offered in explanation but to their symbolic identification with Sun and Moon, and to the sacred significance of Sun and Moon in the new astrological theology invented by the earliest civilizations . . . Laum states that the value ratio of gold to silver remained stable throughout classical antiquity and into the Middle Ages and even modern times at 1:13-1/2. It is obvious that such a stability in the ratio cannot be

explained in terms of rational supply and demand. The explanation, says Laum, lies in the astrological ratio of the cycles of their divine counterparts, the Sun and Moon.

(*Life Against Death*
[Middletown, Connecticut:
Wesleyan University Press,
1959])

So we do after all have some parallels to look at. Here on the one hand is Time, collective or said to be universal Time, derived astrologically from the movements of the heavenly bodies. This Time is said to be of indefinite though very great length; it is said to be the same at all times, at all places, and for everyone; it is impersonal, and yet able to bring about the most decisive effects on persons, making them be and cease from being. Is it a fiction? The analogy compels us to allow for the possibility of its being a fiction, even though the fiction may be founded on a reality (all fictions are, aren't they?).

For here on the other hand is money, collective and said to be universal even though differing in name and form from one land to the next; also derived astrologically from the relations of heavenly bodies. Its amount is thought to be indefinitely large—is there enough money in the world to buy it? the question is like another: is there enough time to make up eternity? and the answer to both is no—and it is said to have the same meaning, or value, for everyone at all times, though this is plainly a superstition; it is impersonal, for there is no difference between your dollar and my dollar, and yet it is able to produce the most decisive effects on persons, even to making them be and cease from being. It is more plainly than time a fiction, yet no one in the least makes any doubt of its utter reality, which consists, perhaps, in its power of conferring reality on things and persons or withholding reality from things and persons.

Now this marvelous figure, Time is Money, has a significant property: it is not drawn from the realm of space, and it is the only figure we have so far found that is not drawn thence. No matter that both time and money themselves may be derived from spatial movements of sun and moon; the figure relating them, or identifying them, is not. For this reason alone it deserves to be elucidated as far as possible.

I remind you here that what I am attempting is not in the realm of philosophizing, except in the most general way, but in the realm of poeticizing, or of poetry considered as a more or less independent mode of thought, what James Dickey called 'metaphor as pure adventure.' In this kind of adventure it is quite permissible, and even necessary, to say foolish things and things contrary to good sense; the only strict rule is that you must follow where the figure leads, you must find out in how many ways it is capable of being interpreted even if some of the ways involve contradictions to experience. So the point now is to accept as fully as possible the metaphor Time is Money, and draw out of it as many of the linkages hidden in that 'is' as possible. Both time and money are ways of enumerating, graphing, placing, and valuing; of introducing minutest regularities into a world whose gestures at regularity otherwise exist, and indeed on the grandest scale, but also with an aristocratic or divine disdain for minuteness in reckoning, such as day and night, ebb and flood, systole and diastole, recurrence of seasons, and so on.

Both time and money appear to be priestly inventions. As to money, 'It has long been known,' says Norman O. Brown, 'that the first markets were sacred markets, the first banks were temples, the first to issue money were priests or priest-kings' (*Life Against Death*, p. 246). And Mircea Eliade, drawing on other authors, tells us that templum and tempus are etymologically related, and even what the relation is: 'templum designates the spatial, tempus the temporal aspect of the motion of the horizon in space and time' (*The Sacred and The Profane*, p. 75, translated by Willard R. Trask [New York: Harcourt, Brace, 1959]). Priesthoods since Chaldean and Babylonian days have been keepers and interpreters of the sacred calendar (the Mayans made theirs out for thousands of years into the future . . . thousands of years, that is, in which no Mayan would be around to read them), and we suppose it is no accident that when mechanical clocks make their appearance it is as if by natural right in the church tower that they do so. Spengler tells us, indeed, that the mechanism of the chiming wheel-clock was invented by a Pope (Sylvester II), and calls this 'dread symbol of the flow of time' 'the first symptom of a new Soul' (*Decline of The West*, translated by Charles Francis Atkinson [New York: Knopf, 1950] I, pp. 14 and 15n.).

Nor have time and money ever lost their original sacred character; in effect their availability to secular enterprises, indeed their absolute necessity to secular enterprises, has if anything made their sacred character of greater authority than ever. Not merely that we date our years from the birth of Christ and dedicate them to the Lord (the scientific-sounding substitution of plus and minus for AD and BC does not seem to be taking hold even among the learned), nor that we inscribe on our moneys the divine name; nor that the architecture and interior arrangement of banks makes them out to be flat cathedrals; nor that the most precise of our ever more refined clocks are kept—for scientific reasons, of course—sealed away from dust and air and from profane glances; sealed, almost, away from time itself. No, in more essential than symptomatic ways, Time and Money are the gods of this world, and when I look about for a third to make up the trinity I think I find it in Number, which is as it were the Holy Ghost that breathes its love from Father Time to Money the Son and Sun and Intercessor in the doings of men.

Is this too arbitrary? I think not. For it was in the first place, if a trinity can have a first place, Number, and the power of enumerating, that made possible Time and Money, as perhaps the God of the Old Testament plainly saw when he forbade the taking of a census, made possible the scientific treatment of every item in the universe including human beings, who from integrities consented to become integers, the difference being perhaps just that between Latin 'individual' and Greek 'atom' its equivalent (and both names conferred equally in error as to the undividableness of either man or atom, which remained for our happy century to demonstrate so resoundingly for both).

Now I stress again that Time is Money is a metaphor, and a metaphor has no intention, any more than it has the power, of being an identity. Yet I think that if, having looked at the ways in which the metaphor works, we now turn to whatever is discrepant in the relation of time and money, we may also learn something.

It was the basis of Rilke's rueful joke about Nikolai Kuzmich that money can be saved and time cannot. That is a plain and apparently irreconcilable difference between the two. But the joke says also: if time *could* be saved, it would be in the form of money. So I propose the following variation by way of hypothesis: the invention of money had and has the unconscious object of inventing a species of time with properties of permanence and ready availability that make it at least seemingly more attractive to human beings. Seemingly, I say, for the story of Midas tells us what actually resulted from this invention. Money is time given permanent form—though of course only for a time. That it is only for a time is no objection in itself; so are all the permanencies of man, and as I said before, all fictions are grounded in realities, just as immortal life is grounded in death.

So our metaphorical proposition now expands as follows: Money, apart from its undoubted other uses, has the purpose of making those who have it feel at ease in the world, just as they would like to feel at ease in time, and as they could feel at ease in time if only time could be freed of its unfortunate directional property, which makes it keep disappearing out the back door just as it comes in at the front.

It may of course be the obverse and hidden point of Rilke's fable, that even if time could be treated as money the accumulation of it in large lots would not serve the purpose of making the time-wealthy man more at ease in the world, but would drive him relentlessly, as Midas was driven, to further accumulations.

EXCEPTIONS AND RULES

A simpleminded proverb, much heard of in my youth, said: The exception proves the rule. At least, it certainly looked simpleminded until I began to turn it over and around and take it apart, when I had to realize there were at least three ways of understanding it.

Some people read the word 'proves' as having the sense of 'tests' or 'tries out,' and if you read it that way (which I suspect was the original intention) the statement is plainly a scientific one. But I noticed in earlier days (back when there used to be proverbs) that people who used this statement in daily life commonly meant something quite different, even contrary; by a change in the meaning of 'proves' the proverb had come to mean to those people that an exception showed the rule to be right. In that sense the statement is nonscientific, or even antiscientific, for to the scientist the exception would show either that the rule was not inclusive enough or that the rule was just wrong, or wrongly applied.*

In that sense, too, the statement is antipoetic, because the poet has still a third meaning for 'proves,' and would say, as a fair statement of his belief, The exception turns out to be, or proves to be, the rule. I shall return to both the scientist's and the poet's reading of the proverb after a bit, but first I want to describe a little more carefully what I have taken to be the common acceptation of the proverb in daily life, where the exception shows that the rule is right, and in that way is said to prove the rule.

Proverbs, which have a way of being antiscientific and antipoetic at the same time, nevertheless have a certain practical shrewdess to them, which we need not dignify with the name of wisdom, but to which we ought to pay some attention anyhow. My sense of this proverb is that it speaks with the voice of authority, as from olders to youngers, from a parent, say, who knows that life is not always explicable, to a child who

---

*Though in the world of microphysical phenomena, in transactions covered by the law of large numbers, 'exceptions' are assumed into rule, or cause, considered as statistical aggregate.

still hopes it is always explicable. For instance, in autumn a father and son are standing under a tree. The son says, Daddy, what are all these leaves? Daddy says, correctly enough, that they are oak leaves. The son picks up a ginkgo leaf and says, Why is this oak leaf shaped so funny? At some nearby point in the ensuing discussion Daddy may say, rather heavily, that it is the exception that proves the rule. And indeed there is no disputing the rule that all those leaves came from the oak, except the one ginkgo leaf, which a passerby happened to have been looking at while out walking and carelessly dropped there when he tired of it, not knowing, or not caring, that he had deranged the order of the universe. You would not say, either scientifically or poetically, that the one ginkgo leaf proved the rest to be oak leaves; but as a way of getting around and through the complications of life in this vale of tears the proverb seems to have been a help.

As the proverb speaks with a voice of authority, so the sense of its somewhat complacent morality is that it is a ruling-class proverb, much concerned with keeping the status quo; no trifling discrepancy, it seems to say, is going to change *my* idea of the world. And the authority assumed is so well established that there is even a little humor to its assertion, as though to allow that you can't spend your life accounting for every last little item in the universe, you've got to stop somewhere, and so on. Its variously elaborated applications in politics and morality might concern us, though, in such forms as 'the sinner testifies to the divine mercy,' 'by his crime the criminal attests to the majesty of the law,' or, drawing on Blake, the magnificent assertion: 'To be an Error & to be Cast out is a part of God's design' ('A Vision of the Last Judgment,' in Blake, *Complete Writings,* ed. Geoffrey Keynes [London, Oxford, New York: Oxford University Press, 1969], p. 613).

An interlude. Just for the sake of the amusement of bewilderment it may be worth following to the end, which is not far away, the formal implications of the proverb.

The exception proves the rule.

But that statement is itself a rule, stating that the exception proves the rule; has that rule also an exception?

Let us assume that there exists a rule without exception. That rule without exception would be an exception to the rule that the exception proves the rule, and as such, by being an exception, proves the rule that the exception proves the rule.

But, on the contrary, a rule without an exception cannot be proved, and if it cannot be proved it cannot be admitted to be an exception to the rule that the exception proves the rule, and if it is not an exception to that rule then it cannot be the exception that proves the rule that the exception proves the rule, and that rule in turn cannot be proved.

So much for that. The head, in testimony of its living in a round world, slowly begins to spin. But I put in that piece of logical parody, or parodied logic, as a humbling reminder that all that we think we think depends upon language, language that already exists before we think, and in which we inherit, in the measure that we are capable, human wisdom and human folly at the same time.

You can see something of this, something of what language does for us and to us, from the circumstance that the one word 'proves,' in what looked to be a simple enough statement, turned out on inspection to have three different meanings making possible three quite different statements of the proposition that the exception proves the rule; but that through these transformations of meaning, which I have divided up as commonsensical, poetic, and scientific, the sentence itself remains formally coherent and grammatically the same.

The poetic form of the proverb asserts that the exception proves (to be) the rule. I found this out as a sort of inexpensive revelation that came to me when I was nearly run over by an ambulance; picking myself up out of the snow I said: Metaphor is an exception caught becoming a rule. For to be even nearly run over by an ambulance is a strikingly exceptional occurrence (though becoming less so), and yet it may be applied accurately enough to the dual nature of civilization, always ready with the instruments of compassion once the victim has been made helpless. Alternatively, the figure may be applied to the situation of the accused, who under our law has the right to be deemed innocent until he is proved guilty; but this right has no actual existence until someone has deemed him guilty by arresting him. Blake again sums it up:

> *Pity would be no more*
> *If we did not make somebody poor;*
> *And mercy no more could be*
> *If all were as happy as we.*

> ('The Human Abstract,' in *Songs of Experience*, ibid., p. 217).

To elaborate a little on this theme, I think many writers would agree with what I have experienced, that very often you are afraid or embarrassed to put down something because it comes directly from your own life, and hence appears to you as too intimate, too idiosyncratic, too aesthetically inert, ever to illustrate any general nature in things. But if you overcome your timidity or shame and put it down anyhow, you will very likely find that it puts out many filiations with the experience of others, the nature of life; it grows, in addition to its being, a meaning, or several meanings.

This is a mysterious business: how does the particular, in the course of being examined most particularly and for itself alone, as a unique fact existing in the world, become meaningful, become illustrative of general or even universal propositions? It is so mysterious, indeed, that nobody knows the answer, any more than anyone knows how it is that things become thoughts and thoughts things. But I may illustrate it as it happened by a curtal sonnet of Gerard Manly Hopkins, which illustrates the happening itself and at the same time asserts a theory about it.

PIED BEAUTY

Glory be to God for dappled things—
For skies of couple-colour as a brinded cow;
For rose-moles all in stipple upon trout that swim;
Fresh-firecoal chestnut falls; finches' wings;
Landscape plotted and pieced—fold, fallow, and plough;
And all trades, their gear and tackle and trim.
All things counter, original, spare, strange;
Whatever is fickle, freckled (who knows how?)
With swift, slow; sweet, sour; adazzle, dim;
He fathers forth whose beauty is past change:
Praise him.

The assertion of that poem is that only a religious guarantee is sufficient for the holding together of fact and meaning, unique and universal. But observe too that if you try to do it without the religious guarantee you don't dispose of the problem; the relation itself doesn't even become less mysterious: how can a finch's wing convince you that there exists an All, an Everything, which is somehow the same (the 'Nature') in all things? A scientific guarantee, as for instance that number is the nature of all things, or that the elementary constituents of the universe perceived by the senses are invisible particles, is also not an overcoming of the same mystery, but a different way of asserting it.

For one more illustration, here are some lines in which my definition of metaphor is applied to some drawings by Saul Steinberg:

METAMORPHOSES

The enchanted line, defying gravity and death,
Brings into being and destroys its world
Of marvelous exceptions that prove rules,
Where a hand is taken drawing its own hand,
A man with a pen laboriously sketches
Himself into existence; world of the lost
Characters amazed in their own images:
The woman elided with her rocking-chair,
The person trapped behind his signature,
The man who has just crossed himself out.

All these instances, taken directly from the work of that marvelously ingenious artist, are exceptions, that is, strikingly unique phenomena—which yet express to us something of what we acknowledge to apply shrewdly to the conditions of our life in this world: with a man laboriously sketching himself into existence, for example, we might compare the saying of Ortega y Gasset—Man is the novelist of himself—where what Steinberg gives as a unique image is asserted as a general rule about the relation between imagination and reality.

So the poet would assert our proverb in the form: The exception turns out to be, or proves to be, the rule.

The third interpretation of the proverb is preeminently the scientist's, and for him the word proves means 'tries out' or 'tests'; if the exception cannot be brought under the rule, so much the worse for the rule. And yet the scientist in formulating his hypothesis is not behaving so very differently from the poet in making his metaphor, though the rules and procedures for 'proving' are very different indeed. Here is a somewhat elaborated expression of our proverb, by Teilhard de Chardin, who says:

An irregularity in nature is only the sharp exacerbation, to the point of perceptible disclosure, of a property of things diffused throughout the universe, in a state which eludes our recognition of its presence.

(*The Phenomenon of Man,* translated by Bernard Wall [New York: Harper, 1959]).

That statement about exceptions and rules was made by a scientist who was also a priest. Hard to be certain whether he says this, in the course of his brilliant and speculative book about evolution, in his character as scientist or in his character as priest. If he said it as a priest, he might well have been defending the occurrence of miracle, which is defined in the great dictionary as follows: a miracle is 'an event or effect in the physical world beyond or out of the original course of things, deviating from the known laws of nature, or transcending our knowledge of these laws . . .'

But do notice that although the priest will indeed break with the scientist in any argument flowing from this statement, he has not broken yet, for the immensely rapid development of science has had a great deal to do with its concentration on 'irregularities in nature,' events 'deviating from the known laws of nature, or transcending our knowledge of these laws,' and the boldest revisions of hypothesis have been necessary (and are still going on) simply in order to bring 'miracle' once again under the dominion of 'law.' And if Teilhard de Chardin made the statement as a scientist, the position is not vastly different, for attention to 'irregularities in nature,' or to what I am calling 'exceptions,' has brought forth upon the world a good many phenomena that might well have been called miraculous in earlier states of 'the known laws of nature.' For example: electricity, in the eighteenth century, was just such an exception, such an irregularity, good for such parlor amusements as picking up bits of paper on a comb statically charged. Consider the immense and immensely poetic power of the imagination, though belonging not to one man alone but to many, that could play with this oddity, speculate about it, devise situations in which it might yield up more information of its ways, until now it is no longer an exception but something close to the principle of existence, as well as the source of practical powers unthinkably great, which have utterly transformed the world. For another example: slips of the tongue, dreams, jokes—these had been around since the beginning; dreams had always been interpreted, too, whether in a systematic or an ad hoc manner, while the other two had been less regarded. But now, because one man took with the most literal seriousness some form equivalent to Teilhard de Chardin's statement, these exceptional, curious, or trivial phenomena have revealed the existence of a huge realm of the world which before had been suspected only in the passing speculations of poets, the strange stories of tradition and religion, the sinister or grotesque images shaped by painters; and it is not too much to say that the world has been as thoroughly transformed by the investigations of Freud as by the development of electricity.

To sum up. Common sense tells you to neglect the exceptional and live within the known world. But art and science are for a moment one in the injunction, even the commandment, to look first, only, always, at the exception, at what doesn't fit: because, one says, it will turn into the universal while you look; because, says the other, it will show you the way to a universal not yet known.

There is probably a moral in there somewhere, but I am in favor of leaving it in there where I found it. I never saw that people got better for being moralized at, especially by one of the wicked.

ON THE RESEMBLANCES
BETWEEN SCIENCE
AND RELIGION

This is a poetic exercise. I begin by assuming that the evident, large, and significant differences between science and religion, scientist and priest, have been amply acknowledged and endlessly elaborated, so that the characteristic relation between science and religion has been either enmity, that is, polar opposition, or no relation at all (the claim that they occupy mutually exclusive realms of discourse). It will be obvious at once that polar opposites must necessarily have much in common; and as to the other claim, that they divide the world between them, maintaining separate spheres of influence, that is a common interim and compromise solution for polar opposites and may be no more satisfactory or enduring here than it is seen to be in politics.

When two things are said to be opposites, it becomes a duty of the intelligence to look for their similarities.

When two things are said to have nothing in common, it becomes a pleasure of the intelligence to find out what they have in common.

The essential procedure of physical science is the experiment, a compound of hypothesis and observation which will produce the same results for anyone, anywhere, at any time, so long as the conditions and steps of the original are scrupulously and rigorously followed. If the same results are not obtained, either the hypothesis is incorrect or the person repeating the experiment repeated it inexactly in some way. In principle, the first alternative is always possible, for even the most adequately supported and long-established hypotheses are not supposed, quite, to become doctrine or dogma; but in practice, when the physics teacher sets up his apparatus before the class and the predicted result fails to occur he does not commonly announce a revolution in physics but apologizes for his error.

The essential procedure of religion is the ritual, a compound of explanation and observation which will produce the same results that have made the assertions of the original *quod semper, quod ubique, quod ab omnibus,* but only if the conditions and steps of the original are scrupulously and rigorously followed in the repetition. If the same results (prosperity at the harvest, victory in war, protection from calamity) are not produced the fault in principle is always thought to be an incorrect following of the procedures either technically or spiritually (in much the same way as prolonged investigation of almost every air disaster finds the cause in 'pilot error'), but in practice, over long periods, gods do disappear, rituals decay, become modified or transformed, are applied to allegedly different purposes.

The assertion that religious ritual is the product of observation may seem strange these days. But priesthood and its procedures were connected with astronomy (from the beginning), as among the Chaldeans; Lord Raglan tells us that what priests observably do (whatever they claim to be doing) is keep a sacred calendar; and, as Christopher Caudwell said of savages, they dance the rain dance at the approach of the rainy season, not in the dry.

Ideally, the scientific experiment can be performed by any sane person who goes about it in the right spirit, that is, a spirit of obedience to instructions. In practice, however, this is rarely possible, and then only with the simplest procedures. I can verify for myself, perhaps, the existence of interference patterns in light. But I do not own or have access to a particle accelerator and would not know what to do with it if I had. So it turns out that experiments are typically carried out by a separate class of persons trained from youth in experimental procedures; in theory, any young person may belong to this class, but in practice it is standard for applicants to be screened by aptitude tests and by a long, arduous novitiate, during which they learn the esoteric language of their vocation.

In certain sects of an allegedly ecumenical religion, especially those sects which refer their beliefs, correctly or not, to a return to primitive practices, anyone who feels moved by the spirit may say the rituals; in the Old Testament, for example, the establishment of one tribe, the Levites, as priest-specialists is relatively late; it occurs simultaneously with the rigorous codifying of doctrine and the forming of a nation. But after and apart from the primitive, the rituals of world religions are typically carried out by a separate class of persons trained from youth in the procedures of ritual; in theory, any young person may belong to this class, but in practice it is standard for applicants to be screened for signs of a vocation and, if they show such signs, by a long, arduous novitiate, in which they learn the esoteric language in which alone the rituals can be efficacious.

The language of science, mathematics, is esoteric and abstruse but international for its initiates; it refers to a supramundane or purely mental reality; it is in its purest form a language about itself, like music, refined of every worldly consideration and yet immensely powerful when applied to the world. The Fratres Arvali in Rome are said to have done their rites in a Latin so dead that they themselves did not know what its formulae meant (it is also said they winked at one another when they met in the street), and Bertrand Russell tells us plainly that 'Mathematics is a science in which we never know what we are talking about nor whether what we say is true' (quoted in Lucienne Felix, *The Modern Aspect of Mathematics,* p. 53), though the printed page will not record a wink.

Even when rituals are recited in the living language of the communicants, that language is highly specialized by archaic forms, lofty and traditional phrasing, and so on. But in our best example for the purpose of comparison, the Latin of the Catholic Church is esoteric and yet international for its initiates, refers to a supramundane or purely mental reality, is in its purest form a language about itself (note the linguistic problems involved in speaking of three persons as both one and three, or of bread and wine as becoming body and blood), ritually associated with music, and yet immensely powerful when applied to the world (as the same linguistic difficulties, when applied to the world, produced numerous bodies and a great deal of blood).

Scholium. We might pause here to look at music as the model language for both science and religion. Music is like that machine built a few years back by someone in California; it had thousands of moving parts and no identifiable function. The first digital computer (and pedal computer too, for that matter) was the cathedral organ, programmed by J. S. Bach, among others, to exhaust all the possible combinational resources of the tonal language as then understood. The musical language is in one respect observably unique, however: nobody died young and poor of Mozart, except Mozart.

Religion and science both have at least three ways of being understood (or not understood). These ways might be listed (for both) as aristocratic, bourgeois, and proletarian, or (also for both) as esoteric, exoteric, and superstitious. They might be diagrammatically set forth as follows:

1. Mysticism, vision, theology	1. Pure, or creative, science; philosophy of science
2. Morals, the good life, order	2. Technology, progress, order
3. The devil	3. The mad scientist

I should emphasize that my first description of the three possibilities as aristocratic, bourgeois, and proletarian does not assert these as fixed limitations of class; nothing in his own nature will prevent the child of a laborer from becoming a theologian or a theoretical physicist, but either will be a very aristocratic thing for him to become. Nor, obviously, is a member of the middle class condemned to be a bourgeois in religion or in science. Salvation to all that will is nigh, we might say, and so is damnation. Now to specify somewhat more elaborately the description of my three categories:

1. Here is the true source of what is generally and laughably called—with a straight face—the practical world: in the dreams and visions of gentle and profound and imaginative men whose word is peace. These men deal purely and in a humble spirit with the most immense and fundamental forces imaginable, with the simple and ineluctable mystery of The Word, The Logos, The Divine Name, Energy, Mass, Light, Number, and so on. They characteristically give utterance to brief, cryptic, world-transforming statements such as Know Thyself, I am the Light of the World, $E = mc^2$, or .000 000 000 000 000 000 000 000 006 6. . . . x frequency = quantum of energy. It seems rarely to occur to them that such announcements could ever become bloody instructions, and indeed the idea does look improbable. And they have their faithful followers, too, men generally regarded as either insane or disloyal by the establishment.

2. These great spirits have their equally faithful followers in the second realm, too. This is the so-called practical world referred to above, where the Logos descended into matter and crucified there becomes the weapon and the cause. This is the world where the great intuition that number is the nature of all things is translated to say that money is the number which is the nature of all things. It is the world of banners inscribed *Gott mit uns, Dieu et mon droit,* of coinage that reads on one side 'In God we trust' and on the other 'Five cents.'

This is not to say that we, who are largely the inhabitants of this second realm, are personally villainous; it is far more likely that we view ourselves, not incorrectly with respect to our situation in society, as driven by necessities beyond our control or understanding, impersonal necessities, compulsions to realize and exhaust all possibility, compulsions to incarnate in corruptible form everything divined for us by the dreamers of the realm above. Here, in our realm, even in metaphysical respects the middle class, live the great administrators of the Word: St. Paul, Innocent III, Ignatius Loyola, Luther, Calvin . . . I refrain from naming the scientific opposite numbers, who are still alive. But this is the realm in which the power of order is more important than anything else, where love another as thyself necessarily becomes the Albigensian Crusade and $E = mc^2$ is necessarily realized as a nuclear weapon.

But it is also and at the same time another realm, this second one, or it can be more benignly regarded: it is the world of that extremely active god from whom all blessings flow. In science these blessings are technological, and extend from the rather humble electric toaster through the remarkable or even miraculous invention of television and so on to splendors untold. In religion these blessings are a little more metaphorical but at least as real in their effects: our invisible identification with the Father above takes the visible form of our affiliation with the brothers below, and the regular iteration of forms of words that at least assure us we are talking about the same world has the effect of giving society a certain appearance of stability and meaningfulness surely as important to the good life as airplanes that run on time.

This is the exoteric realm, where both science and religion are taught as doctrines, or habits, concerning which no doubts exist that will not be cleared up sooner or later, somehow, by someone. It is the realm preeminently where human purpose is assumed to be known, so that no metaphysical nonsense is tolerated unless it is clearly understood to be exterior decoration.

3. The third realm is, at the simplest, where both religion and science are credited with immediate and magical powers, where their instrumentalities are hypostatized as 'beings'—the realm of overt and unsophisticated demonisms, dynamisms, projections, and introjections. As Bruno Bettelheim says, when electrical machines became familiar and important in daily life, 'influencing machines' became important in schizophrenia (see *The Informed Heart* [Glencoe, Illinois:

The Free Press, 1960], pp. 52–61, for a discussion of the general theme). Here we have the more and less complicated idolatries, parodies of the ones in the second realm, dealing with mad scientists, death rays, machines turning on their makers—all these now within the practical realm, by the way—or, on the religious side, with getting in touch with the dead, with cosmic forces, lucky amulets, astrology, fortune-telling, and so forth. There is perhaps nothing more insane here than its equivalent in the second realm, but here it tends to affect individuals, not whole societies.

To the three ways of being (or not being) understood there correspond, in both science and religion, three teachings: 1. Science for scientists, religion for the religious. 2. Science, or religion, for 'the intelligent layman.' 3. Science, or religion, for children.

1. Where the arcana are opened, much is in doubt; even the most fundamental things are left open to dispute.

2. That is largely left implicit, however, where the mysteries are explained 'in simple nontechnical language.'

3. 'The Wonderful Story of Religion.' 'The Wonders of Science.' Color pictures, enthusiasm.

Two final points of comparison may be briefly stated. 1. Scientist and priest are both in the habit, though they regard it not as a habit but as a duty, of using their professional mystery to confer authority on their private opinions in matters concerning the common good. Religion and science both profess peace (and the sincerity of the professors is not being doubted), but each always turns out to have a dominant part in any war that is going or contemplated. 2. Both religion and science cost a great deal of money, much of which is spent on projects, realizable and not realizable, such as space ships and the Tower of Babel, of which the intelligence is not always or easily perceptible to people in other professions.

POETRY AND MEANING

What I have to say to you is very simple; so simple that I find it hard to say. It is that poetry is getting something right in language, that this idea of rightness in language is in the first place a feeling, which does not in the least prevent it from existing; if it is subjective, which I doubt, it is not 'merely subjective' (as students say, and o dear how often they say it); that this feeling of rightness has largely been lost, if not eagerly assaulted with destructive intent, by people who if they ever wake up are going to find it extremely hard to recapture or even to remember what that feeling was.

One possible, and to me likely, consequence of these simplicities will have to be contemplated; it is that poetry in English is coming to an end. I have hesitated fearfully for a long time before that statement, realizing that coming from a middle-aged poet it will helplessly be heard as one more variant of the common cry of middle-aged poets, 'I had talent once, where did it go?' And yet it seems as though the evidence is massive that not poetry alone but a great deal to do with language in relation to mind is fast approaching an end where it will be transformed into something unrecognizably other. To some of this evidence I shall return later on; meanwhile I can at least show that the thought of such an end or such a transformation is not one I hold all by myself.

To show that the question has been seriously entertained I may cite the instance of H. G. Wells and his last work, a little pamphlet called *Mind at the End of Its Tether*: (London, Toronto: W. Heinemann, Ltd., 1945). It was written just after the Second World War and in the last year of the author's life, and in it this great progressive, humanitarian, scientifically-minded, and positivist intelligence—who had predicted in one work after another so much that has come literally true—turned right round to the opposite and declared that intelligence and world, which had for the length of history run on parallel courses, were now separating, like two ships whose paths diverge in the night, or like two celestial bodies that approach one another only to fall away into illimitable dark. Admitted that Wells was old, tired, mortally ill, we have still to inquire whether he was saying something true, or at least probable enough to be given the steadiest consideration, or whether he was merely expressing one more symptom of his malady.

A. M. Turing once said that the question 'Can machines think?' was too meaningless to deserve discussion, and suggested that the proper short answer was 'Can people?' But he added this: 'Nevertheless, I believe that at the end of the century the use of words and general opinion will have altered so much that one will be able to speak of machines thinking without expecting to be contradicted.' You will observe that to this scientist the point is not that superior machines will be invented, though they almost undoubtedly will be; it is that we will have changed our ways of using words, so that thinking will no longer mean what it did. Indeed, this change may in large measure already have taken place. Hannah Arendt says of this, 'If we compare the modern world with that of the past, the loss of human experience... is extraordinarily striking. It is not only and not even primarily contemplation which has become an entirely meaningless experience. Thought itself, when it became "reckoning with consequences," became a function of the brain, with the result that electronic instruments are found to fulfill these functions much better than we ever could.'

And Owen Barfield, possibly the clearest and most searching thinker of the present time, says—though he calls it a provocative heterodoxy—'I have been coming to feel for some time that imagination, *as an end in itself,* is a vein that has been, or very soon will be, worked out. I am in doubt whether much more that is really significant can be done with it' (*The Rediscovery of Meaning,* Middletown, Connecticut: Wesleyan University Press, 1977, p. 125).

There is at least a funnier way of viewing the matter. Otto Rank says somewhere that it took long ages for soul, or spirit, or what we call mind, to work its way up into the head. In some cultures this vital principle inhabited the soles of the feet—the Buddha's footprint is holy—and in others the genitals, the stomach, bowels, heart, liver, and solar plexus were its abode. But among us for a couple of centuries or more thought is commonly believed to be something done in the head, and its sacred function is protected from contamination by the lower parts of the body by collar and tie; compare the expression 'white-collar worker' for someone whose business is mental.

Considering this progression we might reasonably ask by way of extrapolation where this principle of life has left to go. And the student of such matters might look long and hard at the sudden efflorescence of hair styles, including beards and wigs, among the young in late years. It suggests sadly enough people's coming to the dismayed realization that the only thing about yourself you have the power to change, until you go bald, is hair; and it irresistibly reminds me of that species of scientific thought, becoming every day more common, which observes that hair grows out of the head and goes on to infer that the head is full of hair. We are already assured by science that the head does not contain thoughts or words, but only neurons—to which I suppose the teacherly response would be, 'Which of you neurons said that?'

Turning from this topic for the present, I remark that the spectacle, now some centuries long, of western man patiently endeavoring to reason himself out of thought and read himself out of the universe, would be as fit a subject for a comic poet as for a tragic one, were its consequences not so brutal and so lamentable.

I return now to my first assertion: poetry is a way of getting something right in language, poetry is language doing itself right. This idea came first, as ideas have a way of doing, as a thoughtless phrase. I am a most inefficient teacher of verse-writing—but imagine what a monster an efficient one would be!—and term after term, no matter what resolutions of patience and goodwill I began with, three weeks later I found myself saying to the students about their productions such things as: But it's not right, it just simply isn't right . . . and even more cruelly on occasion: if there's nothing right what's the use of trying to say what's wrong with it? And sometimes I would rhapsodize to my poor class about how poetry was simply language doing itself right, language as it ought to be, language as it was in the few hours between Adam's naming the creation and his fall. The whole art of poetry, I would say, consists in getting back that paradisal condition of the understanding, the condition that says simply 'yes' and 'I see' and 'it is so.' Naturally enough, it doesn't happen often. But it does happen.

My students, accustomed to classes in which their instructors explained themselves, explained literature, and in fact left nothing unexplained that could possibly be explained, and now confronting a teacher who apparently couldn't or wouldn't explain one blessed thing, and especially not the one blessed thing they were there to have explained to them, were understandably puzzled. All the same, they behaved very kindly about it. At most, the ones inclined to philosophize would point out to me that my criterion of rightness could never be defined and in any event was merely subjective.

Meaning I could never *prove* anything was right.

I do have a reply to that objection, though unfortunately it is a rather unwieldy one because it has to include some consideration of our intellectual habits with respect to subjects and objects, or, as Coleridge used to say when drinking, sumjects and omjects.

It was Coleridge, I am told, who introduced the words subjective and objective into our language. Ruskin, who was very funny on the theme, hated the words and said they were foisted on us by a combination of German dullness and English affectation. However that may be, I call it to your attention as significant that whole populations which had formerly been able to express their thoughts without resort to the words subjective and objective—whole populations, by the way, including Chaucer and Shakespeare and Milton—now, less than two centuries after their entrance into the language, can scarcely get through a classroom hour without leaning heavily on them. Students, in particular, appear to experience from their use some kind of magical resolution of any difficulty of thought.

I am not trying to take away these terms, which seem to stand to our intellectual astronauts as spacecraft and space respectively. But I would point out first that though Coleridge introduced the words into philosophizing in English he was far indeed from denigrating thought, feeling, or belief by calling them 'merely' subjective. In fact I came by chance on a place where he does just the opposite and refers to the natural world as 'all that is merely objective.'

The great dictionary is pretty funny, as well as illuminating, on *subjective* as a philosophic word, now obsolete, 'Pertaining to the real or essential being of that which supports qualities, attributes, or relations; substantial; real,' for it adds, after what might be a thoughtful pause, 'objective in the modern sense.' Funny, as the sight of great learning trapped in its words may often be, and illuminating about the great change in the mind of the world from a time when true subjectivity could strictly be attributed only to God, to the present, when saying that something or someone is being subjective means a considerable variety of things, all pejorative, e.g., you think it's so but it's not; maybe, but it's not important; you're being emotional when you ought to be reasonable.

It is by some such process as is represented in the changed meaning of such a word as subjective that the mind has reached its present most familiar predicament, ludicrous and pathetic by turns, whereby a learned discipline begins its course of studies by excluding as far as possible all feeling, including especially the feeling of interest, curiosity, pleasure, delight that prompted the study itself, and winds up several years and thousands of pages later plaintively asking itself about human values and wondering where they are to be found. The entire development is of the greatest historical interest, but in the result, it is rather like the man found by a policeman searching under a streetlight for his lost watch. Did you lose it here? asks the policeman, one would have thought unnecessarily. No, I lost it over there, but I'm looking here because the light's better.

This distinction of the whole world into subjective and objective probably began with Galileo's, and then Locke's, division of the qualities into primary and secondary. The dictionary gives the former as bulk, figure, number, situation, and motion or rest, 'which are in the object as in our perception of it,' while the secondary qualities, tastes, sounds, colors, and so on, 'are modes of our perception induced by some character in the object which does not coincide with the perception itself.' One notices immediately that the primary qualities have the air already of being what are called 'hard facts,' while the secondary ones are already a touch sentimental and unmanly. And the scientific way of developing this distinction had the effect of progressively reducing even the primary qualities to quantity, or number, alone, so that only what is enumerable is effectively regarded as real. With this fateful distinction, which indeed did not rest as a distinction but became a division, much else separated that had formerly been one and the object of a single attention; poetry, for example, in the eyes of most of the world, became 'only poetry.' I shan't pause to drop a tear for 'only poetry,' but would suggest that poetry, and literature generally, may be the last remaining place where that about subjective and objective does not apply; and that an appropriate emblem for this characteristic of literature is the situation you have in *Hamlet,* where the Ghost is neither subjective, for the soldiers can see it just as well as Hamlet, nor objective, for when it next appears Hamlet alone can see it, while his mother can see 'Nothing at all; yet all that is I see.' I've a sense that we all incline by training and study to be like Gertrude about our ghosts. Wallace Stevens poignantly varies Gertrude's line, speaking of 'a mind of winter' and of

> *the listener, who listens in the snow,*
> *And, nothing himself, beholds*
> *Nothing that is not there and the nothing that is.*

> ('The Snow Man,' *Collected Poems* [New York: Knopf, 1955]).

Now there is one great trouble with the intellectual and learned school of approach to the art of poetry; it is a trouble that secretly afflicts, I am convinced, a great part of our thoughts about a good many things, and it is this: we are much too concerned to turn our experience into a result, something tangible, and in the course of doing this we forget what the experience felt like in the first place, and, still more important, how through all our studies we remain related to time in two ways, biographical and historical. This is a simple enough thought, and that may be why it is almost always forgotten, though sometimes I've the feeling of its being deliberately excluded. But it bears importantly on this business of poetry as getting things right in language. For the lover of poetry would never have become a lover of poetry, much less a student of poetry, had he not at first had this feeling of rightness and certainty about some piece of language. That came before all question of study, of English courses, of why it was so; enough that it simply was so. James Dickey writes in an essay that he remembers what first attracted him to poetry; it was the rightness of the expression 'to sweat it out,' in relation to the soldier's experience of war.

That brings me to another point about the experience of the rightness of language, and to another thing that is dreadfully wrong about the idea of poetry as a subject to be studied in schools.

It is most important to any inquiry into this idea of rightness in poetry that we be as candid as possible about our actual relation, of feeling and thought, to the phenomena; and with respect to this problem I begin by observing that neither teaching nor criticism is very often quite candid about this relation. For there is always present a temptation, which we almost always yield to, to make our experience of poetry both more intellectual and more pretentious than it is or ought to be. There is a somewhat comic, somewhat vulgar and mercantile, aspect to our serious and no doubt well-meaning endeavors to convince others and even possibly ourselves that the experience we are getting from poetry is certifiably profound, lofty, sublime, organic, harmonious. . . . even pleasurable. You may supply other adjectives, from whatever schools of criticism, as you care to.

Without denying that our experience of poetry is sometimes one or more of those things, I think it proper to acknowledge that it is not always like that, and may not often be like that. A primary pleasure in poetry is surely something low enough to be beneath the notice of teacher or critic—the pleasure of saying something over for its own sweet sake and because it sounds just right. For myself, certainly, and for you if you will remember how it truly was, the thing said over will not necessarily be A Great Thought, though great thoughts are not necessarily excluded either; it may be as near as not to meaningless, especially if one says it without much attention to its context. For instance, a riddling song has the refrain: Sing ninety-nine and ninety. I can remember being charmed enough with that to say it over and over to myself for days, without ever having a single thought about its meaning except for a certain bemused wonder about how different it was from singing a hundred and eighty-nine.

Or else it may be something proverbially helpful, that you say to yourself when things are going wrong: 'Time and the hour runs through the roughest day.' Perhaps this would not have meant so much to me without the little grammatical oddity of 'runs' instead of 'run.' And here are a couple of lines from the *Comedy* that delight me as much now as they did when I first came across them so many years ago:

> *Cosi di ponte in ponte, altro parlando*
> *Che la mia commedia cantar non cura*

> (*Inferno*, XXI, 1–2)

No deep insight here, nor lofty wisdom; he is talking in effect about what he is not going to talk about, though it is wonderfully appealing to be told that Dante and Virgil said things to one another in Hell that we are never going to know, that is not the whole charm of the lines:

> *So from bridge to bridge, talking of other things*
> *That my comedy cares not to sing.*

> (my translation)

It loses much of its delightsomeness in English; loses that lovely, offhanded strolling lilt that makes the Italian, especially of the second line, so wonderful to say. There's a clue in that, maybe, in that *ambulando* rhythm that imitates the two poets walking along; for Paul Valéry gave perhaps the shortest definition of poetry recorded: it is what it says.

One more example. I sang to my children a nursery rhyme I must have missed in childhood:

> *Fiddle dee dee, fiddle dee dee,*
> *The fly has married the bumble bee.*
>
> *Said the fly said he, will you marry me*
> *And live with me sweet bumble bee?*
> *Said the bumble bee, I'll laugh and sing*
> *And you'll never know I carry a sting.*
>
> *Fiddle dee dee, fiddle dee dee,*
> *The fly has married the bumble bee.*

I don't know in the least what there is about this that made me so happy I went about the house chanting it for days on end, in all sorts of situations. . . . until I observed that when I did my wife was beginning to look sideways at me, as though this little verse was turning into A Dark Thought About Marriage.

Which suggests a further step. It is part of the power of a poem to generate meanings from what may originally be meaningless. Perhaps what I am thinking of as rightness in language is this abstract power, or power gained from being very abstract (as Stevens said a supreme fiction had to be)—the power to handle a great many situations at once, the power of poetry to be somewhat more like a mind than a thought. These apparently trivial examples of things that one repeats to oneself rather as though they were talismans, are they not after all the stuff and substance itself of poetry, and more visibly so for not being so cluttered with meanings that we can't see the things themselves? After all, delight itself may mean nothing. Love may mean nothing. The world appears to have every prospect of never meaning anything again. But love and delight and, so far, the world remain.

In an earlier essay I made a detailed comparison between the mechanisms visible in certain sorts of poetry and the mechanisms of jokes. I found the comparison illuminating even if it would not hold equally for all kinds of poetry (I never claimed it would). But in connection with the question of rightness in language as over against the claim that such rightness is 'merely subjective' it is appropriate to draw on that earlier essay for a moment, in order to say as follows.

1. When you understand a joke, you laugh. In fact, your laughter quite simply *is* your understanding, which doesn't express itself in a separate verbal form.

2. When you fail to understand a joke, in a company where every one else seems to understand it and laughs, you either say 'I don't get it,' or you give one of those fake and feeble laughs which you know everyone else will see through at once. What do you not do?

3. I submit that what you never do in this situation is say that the joke is subjective or merely subjective.

4. If someone explains or interprets the joke to you, your difficulty will perhaps be cleared up, but too late; you won't laugh as hard as you would have, had you understood immediately, that is, without the mediation of more words.

5. Therefore a joke is a way of getting something right in language.

6. A poem too is a way of getting something right in language, save that the proper response will be not laughter but silence, or the acknowledgment that it is so, it is as it is; that the miracle has happened once again: 'something understood,' as Herbert says finally and ever so quietly about prayer.

7. It is in this sense that poems ought to be approached as sacred objects. One expects not so much to learn them as to learn from them. They give a certain definition to experience, and it may be that it is to experience we should refer them, rather than to exegesis. By contrast, definitions given in dictionaries break up experiences into units in order to make them—the units, unhappily, not the experiences—easier to understand; but dictionary definitions will at last be found to be circular, hence not definitive, while a poem is 'the burning bow that once could shoot an arrow out of the up and down' (Yeats).

You will no doubt have been thinking for some time that this is all very well, but when are we to have an example? other than, of course, those agreeable trivialities he quoted a few minutes back. But I have deliberately withheld examples because I want the idea of rightness to be as open, contentless, empty if you like, as may be. For I am not at all certain it is so important for each of us to have the same ideas about the same things, even if it is that particular species of what Lovejoy called 'metaphysical pathos' that more than anything else informs and sustains the university and the culture. What is important to each of us is to have the idea of rightness, to grasp it feelingly. If we do not have it, perhaps poetry is not for us; music goes on though many are tone-deaf and few have absolute pitch; absolute pitch has never been accused of being subjective on that account. If you are in the presence of a greater vision than your own—Shakespeare's for instance—and do not see what he is talking about, you don't say he sees nothing, for that would be like telling a microscope that it exaggerated.

In keeping with a somewhat oriental style of going at a subject, a style that abstains from saying what the subject is directly, but hopes to produce an immediate vision of it by indirect means and dark hints—this negative approach is usually translated as 'no-knowledge,' and commentators warn us not to confuse it with 'no knowledge'—I shall present, instead of examples of rightness in poetry, a couple of examples in which, as far as I am able to see, nothing went right at all.

The first is by a student, who has generously allowed me to make use of his effort. In fact it was this student who kindly put me straight by telling me that my idea of rightness was purely subjective.

OPUS 125

The hall of deafness still had heaped
a confusion of memories,
a pile awaiting craftsman's wit;
but he wished he could hear his sobs
when pain forced and hacked into tears,
or, the huge laugh like a giant's
that knew that after all it was
hard work setting sounds in order . . .

I forbear to quote the remainder. I don't want to make fun of it either. It's sad. You can see it's about Beethoven writing the Ninth Symphony, and you can feel that it is very sincere, but it's awful. I said to the student, who by the way is a very intelligent one, 'Here you are, you've read and probably understood half the literature of the past four hundred years—but you've never heard anything.' Maybe the motto of the English Department could be this line varied from Eliot:

We missed the experience, but we had the meaning.

My second example of getting it wrong is professional work, so far as poets may be said to be professionals. Anyhow, it appeared in Poetry Magazine, a title in which, I have often thought, the word 'poetry' has exactly the force that the word 'beauty' does in the title 'beauty shoppe.' Beyond that, not wishing to be invidious, I shall not identify the author; the following is how he begins a piece of some sixty lines:

> A small voice is fretting my house in the night
> A small heart is there . . . Listen,
> I who have dwelt at the root of a scream forever,
> I who have read my heart like a man with no hands
> reading a book whose pages turn in the wind,
> I say listen, listen, hear me
> in our dreamless dark, my dear.

If I read that in a sufficiently sonorous and reverential tone, some of you will doubtless have thought it beautiful, but you are wrong. (It is best, I think, for me to say such things plainly and without qualification.) That is one of the unmentioned and possibly unmentionable dangers to poetry recitations, that any old garbage will go down all right if it's read with conviction.

About that passage I shall comment briefly. For if silence is the appropriate response to rightness, it may be that the real use of talk is about wrongness.

To read the book of the heart is an ancient, conventional expression, hence not good enough for our poet, who wishes to be simultaneously intense, complex, rhapsodic, and desperate, not to mention modern. Still, he is unable to resist this honorable old figure, the heart as a book to be read. So he fancies it up a bit. The speaker is reading the book of the heart? well, chop off his hands at the wrists to show that this is no easy matter; now, to clinch the point home, spring up a wind and start the pages of the book flapping; compared to the speaker's problems here, it would be a cinch for him to dwell at the root of a scream forever. This poetry is intense, indeed, with the grim intensity of someone trying to masturbate too soon after having masturbated.

Maybe from examples such as these we can see the beauty even of wrongness, that from it we infer that a right way of doing things does exist, even that many right ways of doing things must exist, even as from the idea of getting lost we infer the existence of roads and destinations.

I began by saying that I thought this idea of rightness had largely been lost, or destroyed, and that on that account we might have to contemplate the end of poetry as we have known it. And I promised to return to that thought and the evidence for it, knowing that everyone likes a bit of an apocalypse to finish on.

It is a sound maxim for a prophet to hold before him, that when he is about to peer into the future and say that something awful is going to happen, he might well turn around and ask himself if it hasn't happened already. Blake said of this, that prophecy meant simply, If you go on doing thus, the result will be thus. And I add that my favorite prophet is Jonah both for being short-winded and for being wrong about the destruction of Nineveh, that great city wherein, says the Lord in one of his infrequent jokes, are more than sixscore thousand persons that cannot discern between their right hand and their left hand; and also much cattle. Which a poet once brought up to date as follows:

> The Lord might have spared us the harsh joke;
> Many that live in Nineveh these days
> Cannot discern their ass from a hot rock.
> Maybe the word 'cattle' refers to these.

I hope that I, like Jonah, am wrong; though if I should be I too might be displeased exceedingly.

There is a sense, utterly true but not very helpful, in which everything is always ending and always beginning. The fabric of the generations simply is woven that way, seamlessly, and only the work of the historical intellect divides it up. Imagine someone living through the fall of the Roman Empire in a provincial town, in Marseille say, or London; he would live his life day by day, as we all do, and never know that he had lived through the fall of the Roman Empire. He would notice, perhaps, certain signs of neglect; the garrison might go slovenly and unshaven, the roads might not be so well kept up, proclamations would be fewer than they used to be . . . and when people began to notice the absence of something called The Roman Empire they nostalgically replaced it with a Holy Roman Empire and pretended it was the same thing, sort of. So it may be with my subject. I will present my evidences as best I can.

For one thing, the posture of the literary mind seems these days to be dry, angry, smart, jeering, cynical; as though once people had discovered the sneaky joys of irreverence they were quite unable to stop. This is one typical process of Shakespeare's tragedies, where the intelligent and crafty young destroy the stupid old and, with them, the sacred something that these complacent dodos by some accident had in their charge, and the intelligent and crafty young at last, as Ulysses says, eat up themselves.

This symptom in itself is perhaps not much. Literary quarrels have usually been acrimonious, indeed are less personally spiteful now than in the Age of Pope. The world has always been as full of people plugging their friends as of people unplugging their enemies. Yet the public discussion, the criticism, that attends on poetry, has appeared to me as coming close to the point at which a smart shallowness and verbal facility will jettison meaning altogether; the same thing has been happening in poetry itself. I shall not now give examples, but I ask you to consider whether it is not as I have said. Not only the terms of abuse, but more importantly the terms of praise, appear in a language whose vagueness of sense is closely related to the extravagance of its claims.

This kind of shrillness may be the sign of considerable unacknowledged anguish of spirit. As though everyone felt some big thing was breaking up, and made bigger and louder noises to pretend that all is as it was. For it ought now to be possible to turn and look back over the modern period, as it foolishly goes on being called, and see how some one thing—I should date it perhaps from the middle of the last century, from Baudelaire and Swinburne, say—was gathering momentum in a direction and was assembling armies of adherents, but that not so long ago this momentum, giant as it was, divided itself among the members of the armies, diminished, and may now be flickering out in brief contingencies.

I don't know just what name would be right for this momentum. It had to do with a slow collapse in the idea of meaning which progressed simultaneously with an imposing acceleration of the rate at which knowledge was accumulated. Everyone who thinks much about poetry will have observed how in the early years of this century it abruptly became much harder to understand. Not all of it, by any means, but I need mention only Eliot, Pound, Hart Crane, as instances. By heroical efforts of criticism and exegesis Eliot's poems, which seem to have impressed many of their first readers as being written in Linear B, were made part of the common language, so that even ball games now may end not with a bang but a whimper. The same process has not happened to the *Cantos* of Ezra Pound, and I incline to doubt it will happen.

What I am calling the slow collapse in the idea of meaning, which made poetry so very hard to understand and consequently conferred on English Departments a large part of both their real and spurious importance, evidently did not happen in poetry alone. It happened even more conspicuously and at about the same time in physics, in painting, in music; the whole world suddenly became frightfully hard to understand. And there is a corollary to this that I find most interesting: the mind responded magnificently to the challenge of all this difficulty in ever so many ways. . . . and from asking concerning the meaning of this poem or that went on to ask concerning meaning itself. Again, I need mention only a few names: Kenneth Burke, William Empson, I. A. Richards, all seem to have begun by inquiring about the meaning of poems and then to have felt themselves irresistibly drawn to the question beyond: what is meaning, and how does it happen to arise? And the new science of linguistics here enters the picture. Men are now beginning to understand, doubtless as yet in a fumbling and vague sort of way compared to what may be coming, what sort of entity a language is and what relations, of possibility and of limitation, it has to thought. Realizing that language is an abstract and utterly arbitrary but totally articulated system of relations, men now begin to see that they may invent other languages for other purposes—indeed, they do so already.

Anthropology too, with its close relations, folklore and comparative religion and mythology, gets into the act, and for the first time men begin to have a clear and coherent understanding of how literature arose, and what it is, and even a little what it does.

Now these are very real and reckonable advances. I am not antiscience, though I do think that our ways of thinking about what science does and is doing are inadequate and even stupid, and I am not against the accumulation and coordination of knowledge. But I think it is clear that to understand a given matter will have its effect on doing. Students of what is called nowadays The Creative Process do not observably turn into artists. And when the depths of things are exposed to the dry light of reasoned explanation, they may well dry up. For it is paradoxical, and therefore in a round world true, that a great deal of knowledge may come to resemble a great insanity. That may be why I am forced to contend that a vast increase in knowledge was simultaneous with a slow collapse in the idea of meaning.

It is commonplace to observe that we today are the beneficiaries and victims of more language than any people has ever been subjected to in the history of the world. Even going for a walk or drive in the country, we see that the landscape more and more carries written messages—signs. Two strange and related consequences come from this circumstance.

For one, the public language of press and the other media imposes upon us a public dream, a phantasy written in a language that is neither right nor wrong but, say, serviceable. Not so much that it tells us what to think, though it tries to do that as well, but it makes of no avail our freedom of thought by telling us what we must have these thoughts about, and by progressively and insensibly filling us with a low, dull language for thinking them.

The second consequence seems to be that the languages of art and of learning grow ever more recondite, as if they were the distorted mirror images of the public language, which they relate to, more or less as a dream relates to a newspaper.

Yet here too the opposites coincide, for the public dream that is the daily dream of all appears as no less insane, and no less under the threat of an ultimate meaninglessness, than the private dream that is the nightly dream of each alone. And if the languages of the arts and sciences grow progressively harder to understand, the matching phenomenon on the other side is that in the public language it is getting progressively harder to say anything that refers to reality.

I think I can now give a name to the period that is over. I shall assert that it lasted from the middle of the last century to the middle of this one, and I shall call it The Age of Art, or The Aesthetic Age. Its dominant characteristic was the claim that salvation was by art alone. What that salvation would be, or would be like, was specified in ever so many different ways by different artists, but it scarcely ever failed to be asserted that the way and the truth and the life was by art.

Matthew Arnold has often been rebuked for suggesting that art would be the religion of the future, but if you take his statement not as a slogan to wave but as a statement of what was going to happen, it would seem that he was historically accurate, or prophetic.

And if you ask why I hazard a guess that the great period of art may now be over, I can but suggest that, while holding that idea firmly in mind, you look around you. And I would remind you that even if I am somewhat right about what is happening, it may not be altogether a disaster. The world is a very deep place, no matter how much of it we explain, and explain away, and the end of a particular form of experience does not mean the end of experience. Forms are there to be transformed, and of all this something kind and good may come one day. Or so I hope.

THE DREAM OF DANTE

The dream nowhere says it's about Dante, it doesn't even mention his name, nevertheless I woke up knowing it was. It came at a time when I was desperate over an essay about the *Comedy* that wasn't going at all well, and I was saying such things to myself as 'If we go on like this right to the deadline we'll have a hundred and fifty single-spaced pages and no essay on Dante.' It is true, however, that I go through these agonies with any and every piece of writing that cannot be completed in a day; so maybe this dream, which I apply to the piece on the *Comedy,* means to be paradigmatic about my troubles in this line generally.

We are having, it seems, an emergency, but one which ought to be handled with great ease, for we have a stretcher and ambulance (the scene is a garage), and the hospital itself is visible just across the street. (Who is the patient? That remains undisclosed.)

Instead of the obvious and easy solution, however, I find myself upstairs with two or three other people confronting a big, shabby truck, which, moreover, carries atop its cab a sort of thick rug or mattress about the size of a tennis court. We get this latter object down and folded, then it seems we have to strip the truck into parts small enough to carry downstairs so that we can assemble it again elsewhere. And this we do, under the supervision of a bald, squat German who is understood to be a professional mover. We have to pass through a second floor which is evidently the warehouse of a museum or antique shop, crowded with junk from the ages, chiefly furniture, pedestals for statues, and so on.

Outside at last, we are on a football field. More people keep arriving to help put the truck together, and when at last this is done everybody gets in and I am obscurely aware that now there will be no room for whoever the patient was, but this doesn't bother me much at all. What does bother me, though, and bothers everyone else, is that the radiator cap won't stay on. I fiddle with it and discover it is so dilapidated it has no thread on the screw. But I hold it precariously in place with my finger.

Dearly beloved, the patient who never appears and eventually gets forgotten altogether is Dante Alighieri, and I very much fear that the name of the German professional mover is Scholarship, while the truck, of course, is Scholarly Apparatus, a theme reiterated in the warehouse of museum or antique shop. The dream as a whole reflects my nervousness about tackling the great work head on—is that why a football field appears?—as well as, perhaps, a certain sense that the world does not stand in dire need of one more essay on the *Divine Comedy*. My defense, and this is not the first time the thing has happened, is to pretend earnestly to be a scholar, which I am not, and try to sound learned throughout perhaps a dozen false starts, before getting down to being my mere self again, and simply saying what I think. All that is figured by the business of taking apart the truck—and that damn mattress— carrying the pieces downstairs through a collection of antique dreck which perhaps stands for footnotes—there are four editions of the poem on my office desk and two more, different ones, at home—and putting it all back together elsewhere, with the help of a growing throng of scholars; while the concluding image, of the damaged radiator cap which I hold down with my finger, merely shadows forth my sorry-cynical belief as to the probable result of all my efforts.

Even the assertion that 'I go through these agonies with any and every piece of writing that cannot be completed in a day,' though appearing above, belongs to the dream-thoughts, for one of the things which chiefly amazes me about Dante is his successful determination to complete a huge design, a true life task lasting many years:

> *il poema sacro*
> *al quale ha posto mano e cielo e terra,*
> *si che m' ha fatto per piu anni macro. . . .*
>
> (*Paradiso* XXV. 1–3)

as he says with a kind of divine chutzpah redeemed only by his being quite right.

This is a power of poetry, a power of mind itself, far beyond what I could have imagined without having the proof of the poem to hand. As if he had said to the Muse—dared to say to Polyhymnia, Muse of Sacred Song—'Lady, you show up at nine every morning for a decade and more, and I'll let you know when we're finished.'

Struggling with the thoughts that were to make this essay, which had been giving me a bad time for a couple of weeks, it happened that I took the children to a night game. But Dante's poem, for anyone working with it closely, has the power of infecting a good many thoughts about things that would seem quite remote from it, so that when on some occasion of local triumph I saw on the electric scoreboard a bright red cardinal swooping madly up and down and across, I thought: O dear, that's the trouble, isn't it? I mean, that Cross in the heaven of Mars, the imperial Eagle in the heaven of Jove, the ladder in the heaven of Saturn, all made up of spirits who are lights (after you get up past Justinian in Canto VII they no longer have human faces)—we can actually do, or show, these things. That scoreboard could as readily flash out to us glowing crosses and ladders and eagles as it can that cardinal or the pitcher of pouring golden beer which will likely come next . . . and what a vulgar reduction it is. Surely poesy rules in the realm of the impossible just because it *is* the impossible; realization is ruin.

But a few nights after, taking the children to the Fourth of July fireworks, and seeing those truly wonderful sprayings and flowerings, those glowing showers of embers slowly going out—they actually do make people say ooh! and ah!—I thought, with a kind of stupid relief, Ah, well, that's more like it, the spirits on cross and ladder come and go swiftly, like the fireworks, brilliant with heat as well as light, and with the continuousness of a musical phrase, *legato* . . . only they don't go out. And I felt better, heaven knows why. For both these comparisons, scoreboard and fireworks, had merely obtruded themselves on my vision of the poem because I saw them while preoccupied with the poem. The poem, however, is to be read with the mind's eye, not the body's eyes, which are the necessary but not sufficient receivers of its words or of its visions.

Still, the poem is near seven hundred years old, and if much has remained the same—including death, cruelty, stupidity, and smiles—ever so much has changed. And, still thinking of cross and eagle and Jacob's ladder, I remembered two quotations bearing on this matter, though written three centuries apart. I'd had them about for some years, and here seemed to be an occasion for putting them together.

> What a beautiful hemisphere the stars would have made, if they had been placed in rank and order; if they had all been disposed of in regular figures . . . all finished, and made up into one fair piece, of great composition, according to the rules of art and symmetry.

That is Bishop Burnet, as it were introducing the eighteenth century. But here is how the same thought occurs to George Santayana, introducing the twentieth:

> . . . imagine the stars, undiminished in number, without losing any of their astronomical significance and divine immutability, marshalled in geometrical patterns; say in a Latin cross, with the words *In hoc signo vinces* in a scroll around them. The beauty of the illumination would be perhaps increased, and its import, practical, religious, cosmic, would surely be a little plainer; but where would be the sublimity of the spectacle? [And he answers] Irretrievably lost.

> (*The Sense of Beauty* [New York:
> C. Scribners Sons], 1896)

It's a matter of your—or your century's, perhaps—taste in universes. Dante's cosmology is as absurd to us as—well, as ours would be to Dante. In effect, he might claim with reason, in spite of all our chains of zeroes hiding behind the exponents, we don't have a cosmology at all, any more than the ancient Maya, who kept accurate calendars extending many thousands of years into a future in which there would not happen to be ancient Maya, could be said to have a cosmology.

Much has changed, yes. On this point, an anecdote.

A student came to his teacher just after commencement, and paid him what at first looked to be, and certainly was intended to be, a tremendous compliment. 'Sir,' he breathlessly said, 'there was one thing I learned in your course that is of greater significance than anything else I have been taught in my four years at this university.' Teacher, bridling prettily, inquired what this wonderful one thing might be. 'Why, that right during John Milton's lifetime the sun stopped going around the earth, and'—he made a twisting motion with his arms—'the earth began going around the sun!'

As a testimonial to effective teaching, that's as pathetic as it's funny. But if that teacher had happened to take his motto from Leibniz—

'there's nothing so stupid I can't learn from it'—he might have gone on to consider thus.

A silly error, yes. But also a convincingly surrealist metaphor about how it might have felt mentally if not physically, that violent wrenching of the frame of things begun by Copernicus and Kepler, Brahe and Galileo. And if you continue along the lines it indicates about the relations of mind and world, you might wonder at other of the great changes since Dante's time, changes having to do with the age of the universe, of the earth, of life, of human life; and changes having to do with the size of the universe, which has grown so exponentially from the little local affair it was to something of a size so unimaginable that it has to be expressed in light years—to give one figure only, our sun and its system lie on the rim of our galaxy 26,000 light years distant from the center, which is to say, being interpreted, the distance covered by light traveling 6,000 billion miles a year multiplied 26,000 times. . . . Can you say with utter confidence whether changes of such quality and magnitude take place in the world or in the mind, whether Aristotle himself would be quite clear as to whether they are recognitions or reversals? So it might be with the Copernican Revolution just as that student said: the sun stopped going around the earth and the earth started going around the sun, with consequences, including the demythologizing of knowledge, the dissociation of cosmos and consciousness, physics and faith, which I am sure you are as much and as little familiar with as I. Much has changed.

But when I look up into the night sky—and no matter how much science insists that the direction of my gaze is out, not up, my neck tells me I am looking up—I see not Dante's neat Ptolemaic universe, nor the elegant Copernican universe that replaced it, still less the vast universe more recently offered us by Harlow Shapley and others; I see, as men always have seen, the appearances which were to be accounted for by these universes; indeed, I don't see very many of them, owing to the smog, which seems to be one of the conditions under which it becomes possible for men in windowless buildings watching television monitors to send travelers to the Moon and Mariners out past Mars. So that although the size of the Milky Way has increased to include an unimaginable and indeed incredible 200 billion stars, it is among the effects of the scientific and technological civilization which makes this and the like assertions that I was unable, at last look—Fourth of July again—to see any Milky Way at all. That's a bit more of the much that has changed.

So Dante's cosmos does indeed look silly, but only until I try to contemplate my own and learn that I don't effectively have one. Not only the smog that prevents me from seeing the stars, but the electric light so effective in demythologizing the world that it shields me from demon and angel alike, and insures that save for the Fourth of July I will not worry enough about the stars to go outdoors and see whether I can see them or not. And not only that, but this: Increased knowledge increases ignorance exponentially, and every triumphant advance in knowing means that millions of us won't know it.

That, perhaps, is poetically the point. Dante has a small universe, but a full one, and he knows it thoroughly. I have, if I can in any sensible way be said to have it, a vast universe, but it is empty and dark, and compared with what is to be known I do not know it at all.

Away from the *Comedy,* I may have my doubts. But while I am reading, the illusion of plenitude is complete; I am convinced. I don't know whether to be more amazed at his faith or at his knowledge, at his humility or at his pride, but when I read the poem I am kept constantly under an enchantment that says, 'Everything you need to know is here.' So much is this so, that when I hear at the opening of *Inferno* XXI:

> *Cosi di ponte in ponte, altro parlando*
> *che la mia commedia cantar non cura,*
> *venimmo . . .*
>
> *So from bridge to bridge, talking of other things*
> *which my comedy cares not to sing,*
> *we went along . . .*
>
> (my translation)

I am amazed all over again to learn that Dante and Virgil said things to one another in Hell that we are never going to be told.

This must be, I think, the supreme illusion possible to poetry, perhaps to any power of the mind, and it makes me think of the *Comedy* as a kind of holography, in which everything is always present at every point. Or of Borges's Aleph; or of a famous remark of Whitehead's, that 'In a certain sense, everything is everywhere at all times, for every location involves an aspect of itself in every other location. Thus every spatio-temporal standpoint mirrors the world.' Or of this that happened between Juliana of Norwich and her Saviour: 'He shewed me,' she says, 'a little thing, the quantity of an hazel-nut, in the palm of my hand; and it was round as a ball. I looked thereupon with the eye of my understanding, and thought: "What may this be?" And it was generally answered thus: "It is all that is made." '*

This illusion of plenitude has to do in the first place with an exact fit between inside and outside in the poet's arrangements. There are in the main two sorts of outside, the articulation of the poem and the articulation of the universe, and they too coincide to give the impression that everything is contained within them and that nothing remains outside them. But then there is the inside, the human action that expands so as to fit exactly with its ordained outward.

The briefest reminder of these articulations ought to do, as they are well known to every reader of the poem. First, the arithmetic, built chiefly upon three and ten. Three canticles of thirty-three cantos each, with one canto for general prologue to the whole, bringing the total to one hundred. The cantos are of varying lengths, but average out so as to make each canticle about the same number of lines, and the poet keeps a strict awareness that this is so, warning himself at the end of the *Purgatorio* that all the pages ordained are filled up, so that the curb of art allows him to go no further; and being similarly warned toward the end of the *Paradiso* that it is time to stop, like the careful tailor who cuts the garment according to the cloth at hand, he stops.

To these purely arithmetical or numerological dispositions the physical and moral natures of the universe conform themselves. Corresponding to the three canticles, the three realms of Hell, Purgatory, Heaven. Each of these is again divided into three main stages of the moral life imaged forth in the architectural arrangements of circles, terraces, and spheres. In Hell these divisions descend in the order of incontinence, violence, and fraud; in Purgatory they ascend in the order of perverse, defective, and excessive love; in Heaven they are represented as raying outward according as the blessed were affected by worldliness (and are accordingly seen within the cone of the earth's shadow) or lived lives of action or of contemplation. Outside of these schemes is another realm of a different order, bringing the total in each canticle to ten: Limbo, the Antepurgatory, the Empyrean.

---

*Revelations of Divine Love, Ch. 5. See the point in the *Paradiso* (XXVIII. 41-2) of which Beatrice says:

> Da quel punto
> depende il cielo e tutta la natura.

The marvelous thing, poetically, is that this scheme is not set forth complete but built up for us by stages of description and reminder until it stands forth in memory with its symmetries and balancings and intricate cross-relations, all deriving ultimately from the mind of God but all, the one and the many, experienced serially as an adventure of the pilgrim through the types of the adventures of mankind generally—*exemplorum positivus,* as he says elsewhere—driven home by examples. And in the mystery of the many examples we are gradually to perceive the mystery of the link between human freedom and the workings of divine necessity, the link between individual and type. It is as Blake described it in a famous passage of *Jerusalem*:

> *All things acted on Earth are seen in the bright Sculptures of*
> *Los's Halls, & every Age renews its powers from these Works*
> *With every pathetic story possible to happen from Hate or*
> *Wayward Love; & every sorrow & distress is carved here,*
> *Every affinity of Parents, Marriages & Friendships are here*
> *In all their various combinations wrought with wondrous Art,*
> *All that can happen to Man in his pilgrimage of seventy years.*

Indeed, Blake, who illustrated the *Comedy,* may even have been thinking of it in these lines, and perhaps especially of the marvelously carved illustrations on the cornices of Purgatory.

So, in a fanciful comparison, the poet is like Theseus, led by the thread of love in such a way that in the journey to the Minotaur he also learns the labyrinth as a whole.

So far we have stressed the architecture, in its correspondence to the articulation of the divine plan, or Necessity. Through this web of geometry, geography, and cosmology, all the creatures move, as Beatrice says, to diverse ports over the great sea of being. But at the very fulcrum of the poem, the middle of the fiftieth canto, Marco Lombardo makes it clear that human beings have freedom from stellar or other necessity; they have minds, which the heavens have not in their charge; hence their salvation or damnation is not under the doom of Necessity, though it will indeed illustrate Necessity.

This is the mystery of individuality itself, and in it the problem of universals is not so much solved as set forth and assumed poetically to be solved.* Against the background of the circles of Hell, the terraces of purgation, the starry wheels of Heaven—all that insane arithmetical

---

*As, in experience, it is always presented as solved; if no solution, perhaps no problem?

regularity as circular as a Kandinsky, which in my moods of disaffec-
tion with the poem make me think of it as *The Rube Goldberg
Variations*—is placed the wild richness and unpredictable particularity
of people on their ways through the dark wood or their moving over the
great sea of being.

Here perhaps is where the illusion of plenitude is most convincing,
or is totally convincing. Dante knows so many people; he knows so
many stories! He seems never at a loss for a story striking in its
individuation, epigrammatic in its allusive concision, and pointed as to
its illustrative quality with respect to salvation or damnation and exact
moral type. This quality chiefly is what led me to say that Dante's
universe, though small in both space and time compared to ours, and
more especially *closed* in both space and time, is a full universe, and one
which he knows thoroughly, is utterly at home in—as one could be
only in a universe which, at whatever size, is closed. The inside exactly
fills up the outside. Hence my impression while reading the poem that
everything is in it.

This impression is reinforced by the multitude of symbolic resonances and redundancies that echo through the work and are the other
side of his striking power of individualizing his figures. Dante's habit
of mind is deeply, almost involuntarily, typological, not only with
respect to the correspondences between the Old and New Testaments
but with respect also to the correspondences between scriptural history and pagan myth and history, and the continuity between both of
these and the history of contemporary Europe. It is in this poetic power
of com-position, literally of putting together, that he is supreme.

He is also the most learned of poets, or the one who, among the
greatest poets, relies the most upon learning and allusion. Side by side
with his magnificent attentiveness to the visual, the power of putting
before us with the utmost plainness what he is seeing, so that we see it
too, there is this other power of riddling diction that is constantly
making us supply more information than the words themselves convey,
and infer whole stories from an image or a line. Consider, in this light,
such things as the sketches of the images of Pride carved on the pavement of Purgatory, where in thirty-odd lines of paralleled tercets he
swiftly reviews a succession of paired examples from Scripture and
Greek myth: Satan and Briareus, the Titans and Nimrod, Niobe and
Saul, Arachne and Rehoboam, Alcmaeon and Sennacherib, Cyrus and
Holofernes, finishing with the ruins of Troy. Or consider the arrogant
virtuosity of Justinian's history of Rome under the figure of the impe-

rial Eagle, sweeping *cito et velociter* back and forth across Europe so as to summarize the span from Aeneas to Charlemagne, about a millennium and a half from the founding of the city, and on to the disputes of Ghibelline and Guelf of Dante's own time, all in eighty lines or less, only for the poet to balance all this gorgeous speed and strength against the story of the humble pilgrim Romeo, a spectacular contrast of pride, power, scope, and speed with a quiet tale of a faithful servant misprized and exiled to beg his way through the world in poverty and age (in which respect he may be, as so many others are throughout the poem, a type of Dante himself). The passage about Rome is thick with famous names to which the reader's memory must supply the stories, and includes even the crucifixion and the destruction of the Temple under Titus, given in a sentence so riddling that its full elucidation by Beatrice takes up the whole of the next Canto.

One last illustration of what I have been calling the illusion of plenitude returns us to that idea of the presence of everything in something, which is of the essence of the art of poetry and which is imaged forth in such stories as that of Juliana and the hazel-nut.

The scheme of the poem is in a certain sense anecdotal and picaresque. Our hero, alone alive among a host of the dead, alone moves on through all the three realms, and there is consequently a temptation to read each episode as entirely separate from all the others, if only because the persons in it will never reappear.

But there is, owing to Dante's power of composition, a further dimension, of resonance, of symbol, of mysteriously allusive interconnection, between this example and that, between the examples and Dante himself, and so on.

Dante sees his poem as a sea voyage, as is well-known; the chief places are the beginning of the *Purgatorio*—

> *Per correr miglior acqua alza le vele*
> *omai la navicella del mio ingegno*

—and near the beginning of the *Paradiso,* with its ominous warning to the reader not to put forth on a sea never sailed before unless he is one of the few who have stretched forth their necks to the bread of angels, a passage followed by an odd comparison to Jason and the Argonauts.*

*See also *Paradiso* XXIII. 67.

Human life, too, is a sea voyage, says Beatrice, over the great sea of being.

Later on, Beatrice mentions, as a warning against believing one has seen deeply into the divine will, having seen a ship complete a long voyage only to be wrecked on coming into harbor; whereupon one can't help hearing a faint echo of the mad voyage of Ulysses, shipwrecked within uncomprehending sight of salvation, the mountain of Purgatory.

Now Ulysses' voyage, very likely invented by Dante, was characterized not only as the *folle volo,* the mad flight in pursuit of knowledge, but also as the *alto passo,* the deep passage, the high adventure, which is the term already applied by the poet to his own pilgrimage.

Such dark prophecy as Lewis Mumford has seen in the technological schemes of Leonardo, as Loren Eiseley in Bacon's summons to the study of nature, as Eiseley and Richard M. Weaver in the apparition of the witches to Macbeth, I seem to see in Dante's story of Ulysses: a story of heartbreaking brightness on the way to doom.

Ulysses wants knowledge, and for knowledge he will break his ties with Telemachus, Laertes, even Penelope, to sail westward through the Mediterranean after escaping the enchantments of Circe, who turns men into beasts. The object of this knowledge? It is at first to become expert in the world, learned in human vice and human worth; but this knowledge is dismissed in three lines of tourism: he and his men saw Spain, Africa, Morocco, Sardinia and some other islands; then, old and slow with age, they come to the straits of Gibraltar where Hercules had set down his pillars as signs to men of limits, that they should go no further. Here worldly knowledge can no longer be the goal, because there is nothing out there, nothing but water. Ulysses exhorts his fellows, in the name of the dangers they have shared in reaching the westernmost limit of the world, to continue in the name of knowledge (*esperienza*) even though, or just because, the knowledge is of nothing, of the unpeopled world behind the setting sun. As if the journey were to begin with what indeed it presently becomes, a journey into death. And again, as if remembering Circe, he concludes what he calls 'this little speech' by reminding them that they were not made to live as beasts but to pursue *virtute e conoscenza.* One of my editors says tersely of *virtute* that it means *il bene,* but perhaps we may see in anticipation here the Baconian coupling of knowledge and power. What knowledge and power may be expected of the void, however, we are never told. Instead, Ulysses conveys rather backhandedly his opinion of his fellow men by saying that the 'little speech' so fired them up that he could not have held them back from what he knows (now, or even at the time?; the text will tell us nothing on this point) to be 'the mad flight.'

So they turn the poop toward the rising sun—given the consistency of the symbolism of the sun throughout the poem, even this navigational detail is a telling one—and row out into vacancy, always bending leftward, to the sinister side; indeed, to the sinister, for this is forsaking the *via diritta* in its bodily form.

And out of all this, after five months, they do achieve a distant view of Purgatory mountain—dark with distance—and are peremptorily struck down by the whirlwind of the divine displeasure, though even now Ulysses knows the will behind the storm only as 'what pleased Another.'

That is the strange story told in dark Hell out of a tongue of fire, a story full of the freshness of sea, wind, and sky, a story of courage, nobility, and strength, and, as it happens, madness. The voyage of Ulysses is a mad flight, yes, but it is also the *alto passo* (the deep passage? the high adventure?) which is the term the poet has already applied to his own journey proposed by Virgil (*Inferno* II. 12). It is like a fleeting glimpse, from the closed and closing universe of the high middle ages, of the coming of the Voyages of Discovery, which themselves were associated in men's minds with the chance of finding the way back to the earthly paradise from which their first parents had, being driven out, driven out all.

But it is more than that. It is also, I think, an account of the *terribilita,* nobility and pathos of the drive toward knowledge that has with an increasing acceleration obsessed the world since Dante's time. Not, obviously, that the men of the Middle Ages were not themselves obsessed with knowledge; if we had Dante's poem for the only evidence of that, it would be enough. But this seems an intuition of the practical knowledge—*esperienza*, our poet calls it—that Bacon would associate with power: the knowledge that imposes upon the knower an ultimate compulsion to know, to experience, to find out, even if the object of the knowledge be nothingness, even if the result of the finding be death and hell.

And when, from high in heaven, the poet turns at Beatrice's command for one of his two marvelous looks back and down at the *aiuola che ci fa tanto feroci,* the little threshing floor of earth that makes us so ferocious, he remembers just in passing that voyage of Ulysses—as though, one feels, it formed some sort of doomed counterpart to his own fortunate and blessed voyage.

Ulysses and the fall of man both relate to knowledge and lust. Whenever Ulysses turns up, three times in all, it is in the company of some sort of sexual enchantment. When he tells his story, he begins with leaving Circe, who had kept him for over a year, and his exhortation to his crew includes a denunciation of bestiality. In Purgatory, Dante dreams of a siren who mentions having enchanted Ulysses just before she is revealed by Virgil as a creature of falsehood and filth. The last memory of Ulysses and his *varco folle,* high in heaven, is companioned in the next line by a reminiscence of Europa's rape. So sexuality, bestiality, and the voyage are brought together in these fleeting and riddling allusions, which echo over great spaces of the poem. And, remembering these things well enough to put them together as a dream might do, we remember that Dante began his journey somewhat as Ulysses did—threatened by bestiality in the form of three beasts, previously guilty of allowing himself to be seduced by both sexuality and knowledge (in the form of philosophy, his own Circe), for which in the Earthly Paradise he will suffer the scornful rebuke of Beatrice—with the sole redeeming difference that Dante is under the protection of faith, the protection of a Lady who is not Circe or the Siren or Europa.

And the vision of the voyage returns once more, with all these various voyages, to form its overtones in a figure of the strangest harmony in all poetry:

> Un punto solo m'è maggior letargo
> che venticinque secoli alla 'mpresa,
> che fè Nettuno ammirar l'ombra d'Argo.

This one moment in the presence of God is both a moment, a timeless Now, and the moving Now of all of human time, and both are made equivalent: It is a greater *letargo*—the word includes both fatigue and oblivion—than all the five and twenty centuries since the enterprise that made Neptune marvel at the shadow of the Argo, the first ship, hence the beginning of the enterprise of history. In this strangely displaced figure the unitive experience of the divine compounds the consciousness of the long fatigue of history with unconsciousness itself, the moment as part of duration with the moment as timeless and already in eternity, and—poetically, at least—the Christian revelation and promise with the ancient pagan god of the sea and with Jason on another of those doomed and damned voyages like that of Ulysses . . . for one remembers already, long ago, having seen Jason, stalking so proudly through Hell that even Virgil admires his royal port; and to have heard of him once again, intruding figuratively into the warning to the reader near the beginning of the *Paradiso,* where the furrow ploughed by the poet's keel reminds him of Jason ploughing at Colchis in the presence of his marveling crew.

Such resonances, whatever they mean—and of their nature, perhaps, our idea of their meaning will be flickering and mysterious as is the meaning of coincidence and relation in life itself—seem to touch upon an essence of the purest poetry in their strange power of balancing, blending, harmonizing many diversities across great and sounding distances, giving a riddling hint of a oneness in the world that for a moment shines through the manifold appearances—the moment, as it were, just before metaphor is born and explanations—such as these helpless ones of mine—begin.

Part Two

SPECULATION
TURNING TO ITSELF

❧ ꜩꜩ ❧

My object is to consider, as simply as I can, sight, language, thought, in their relations. And I observe that the word 'consider' exemplifies these relations right away, for it first meant 'seeing the stars together, as constellations, or in relation to one another,' and so suggests how hard it is to find words for separating out sight, language, and thought long enough to examine their relations—where the word 'relation' might have the narrative sense: telling a story about seeing, saying, and thinking.

Seeing seems to tell us that we are in the world, and that the world we are in is quite real; for without light, seeing is not. The corollary to this is that we too are quite real (for all the reassurance and the helplessness the thought confers); for without an eye, seeing is also not. But the mind—which, nevertheless, with the cooperation of language, is the agency self-appointed to say these things—is never satisfied with that, but seeks helplessly and sometimes in its own despite the completion of the analogy: as the eye to the sun, so the mind to . . . ? and echo answers. Which is not to say that nothing answers, for it may be by a species of radar that the mind moves through the world, blind otherwise as a bat—save that, says Richard Wilbur:

> *in the very happiest intellection*
> *A graceful error may correct the cave.*

('The Bat')

The Platonic theory of vision by emission of light from the eyes broke down on the mere absurdity of nightfall; a tragic instance of hubris getting its come-uppance from on high, as theories of immortality tend to be extinguished by the fact of death—though we note in passing that blindness also comes from staring at the sun—*lux circumfulgens visu privat*—or at the godhead. But it is a lovable theory in its wish to humanize the world, and it seems undeniable that some sort of emission from the eye is necessary to vision, though we do not regard it as physical but as psychic, and call it *attention* rather than light.

In one way, seeing is the model for thought. To say 'I see' is immediately to mean 'I understand.' It is a naive proverb, a proverb of the eye, and the mind very often refuses to believe it; nonetheless, it keeps coming back. And certain very lofty forms of the mind's activity are signally distinguished as being 'above' or 'beyond' mere thinking by the word 'vision'; as though the end of all our intellectual labors were but to return us to plain ordinary seeing something—save that the something seen will here have been something ordinarily invisible.

But before we can settle on 'seeing is the model for thought' as our slogan, something else has popped in between seeing and thinking, and that is language, with its immense power of translation, its strange air of otherness, its way of interposing itself actively not only between ourselves and the world but also between ourselves and what we hope are our own thoughts. For example: I am speaking to you in language, and you are listening (I hope) to me in language. But at the same time I am not trying to tell you language, I am trying to tell you what I think, and (let us hope, again) you are not only listening to language but trying to derive from it what I think. A curious transaction, but we seem to be stuck with it.

So we have to say at one and the same time: 'Seeing is the model for thought,' and 'language is the model for thought.' By our own great efforts we have arrived back at two versions of the beginning: 'Let there be light' from the Old Testament, and 'In the beginning was the Word' from the New. And if the eye should say again its naive proverb, seeing is believing, the mind might reply somewhat austerely that it is a vulgarity, if not a positive contradiction, and in any case of no particular use or merit, to believe in things that you can see. There are robins all over the lawn, but who would bother to believe in robins? No, believing is much harder than that, and was defined once and for all and long ago by a virtuoso in the art: I believe what is impossible, what is absurd, what is in fact unbelievable; like the Red Queen, who practiced by believing as many as half a dozen impossible things before breakfast. For you can believe only what you can doubt, preferably at the same time.

I am trying to stay with my intention of saying only a few very simple things about seeing, language, and thought; but it is hard to resist numerous and charming temptations to digress that beckon everywhere. I yield briefly to one. It is surprising not to find any robust and widespread mythology locating the soul in the eyes, though perhaps we come near to it in the pineal gland, in Donne's 'pictures in our eyes to get / Was all our propagation' ('The Exstasie'), or in its modern equivalent, where the friend of the family says to the child, 'I knew you when you were only a glint in your father's eye.' But onward.

The relation of eye and mind is intimate and contradictory, and maybe language is the element of contradiction. It is the difference between seeing and seeing through. If I glance idly out the window, the world is there; it is not in doubt either that it is there, of itself, or that it is outside. If I try, however helplessly, to think about this situation, the first thought and the last are the same: it is concealing something from me . . . it is trying to tell me something . . . there is some identifiable relation between that out there and this in here . . . Such thoughts may be simple, idle, and lead nowhere: 'What is God doing, shaking the leaves of that tree, trying to get my attention?' Or they may be highly sophisticated and instrumental to knowing, as in the following somewhat extended variation:

> Around the stems and branches and foliage of the nerve-tree is draped a diffusely-connected network. This fringe of uncertain function . . . is associated with simplicity and also with a high degree of adaptability and plasticity. The diffuse nature of the tissue serves to remind us that to deal with uncertainty is the principal function of the higher centres, which must pilot a vulnerable animal through . . . a world where chaos and cosmos are interlaced and superimposed, where anything may happen, but nothing happens twice.

> (W. Grey Walter, 'Activity Patterns in the Human Brain,' in *Aspects of Form*, ed. L. L. Whyte)

In another version of this tree of the knowledge of good and evil, draped with a fringe of uncertain function, William Blake sees it as Tyburn gallows, the deadly Nevergreen, and names it Moral Virtue (*Jerusalem*, 29 f.). In 'The Human Abstract' he describes it as watered by Cruelty's tears, its root Humility, its shade Mystery, its fruit Deceit; 'And the Raven his nest has made / In its thickest shade.' He concludes:

> *The Gods of the earth and sea*
> *Sought thro' Nature to find this tree;*

> *But their search was all in vain:*
> *There grows one in the Human brain.*

This relation of seeing and seeing through is a very poignant one, responsible simultaneously for civilization and for its discontents. And right in the midst of the relation is language, facing both ways, toward things and toward thoughts, toward the visible world and toward all the invisible ones. This is not metaphysics but description, for the invisible does not begin with God, the gods, and such high matters; it begins much closer to home, wherever pattern is discriminated and relationship inferred: no effect, for instance, as Hume said first, has ever been visible in its cause.

So. The sight of the eye rests on the object. The sight of the mind is never satisfied with that, but wishes always to go through the object, relating, transforming, perhaps even eating it so as to make it a part of mind, which characteristically wishes to say of the object: It is an example of, it represents, it stands for, it symbolizes, it means, it is a member of this species of that genus . . . it works in thus and such a way.

For the sight of the eye the world is evident, it is there, it is a surface. For the sight of the mind the world is a secret to be probed, and the fascination of the mind, the fearsome pleasure that holds it to the world, comes from the belief that what we see is never what is there, or never only what is there, but always stands in some shadowing, reflecting, distorting, hinting relation to what is there. What the eye sees, the mind holds to be *appearance,* and sometimes it seems as if the mind's great ambition would be to declare the whole show a false appearance, and to behold it fade into invisibility even as the beholding mind itself swooned into unconsciousness. But that ambition has so far seemed unable to be satisfied short of death, for the appearance, in the mind's myth about it, can never be altogether and only false, because it is only by seeing through it to something else, something beyond, beneath, above, that the mind can delight itself for a moment with the discovery of what it was that the appearance tried to falsify. For a last turn of the screw, you have the mind's deep suspicion that the reality concealed and hinted by all the appearances of the world is the mind itself, which can obtain no view of itself save by going forth into the world and becoming itself an appearance of itself:

For speculation turns not to itself
Till it hath travell'd, and is mirror'd there
Where it may see itself.

(*Troilus and Cressida*, Act III,
Scene 3, 109–111)

Thus Shakespeare, adding casually: 'This is not strange at all.'

This relation, wherein the partners are both indispensable and contradictory to one another, appears to be as old as speculative thought. Perhaps it has never been put more deftly and decisively than in that brief dialogue of Democritus where the mind first speaks loftily to the senses, saying: 'Sweet is by convention, bitter is by convention, everything is by convention. Nothing is, but atoms and the void.' To which the senses, with great indignation: 'Wretched mind! You take from us the evidence with which you seek to overthrow us. Your victory will be your downfall.'

It seems that the mind's characteristic mode of action is to take the vast multiplicity of the visible world and reduce it to a single, not quite all-powerful, pair of terms: atoms and void, concord and discord, eros and thanatos, and—the example which may be the model for the others—father and mother, who when myth passes over into philosophy reappear in a more sophisticated disguise as form, or pattern, and matter. These paired terms between them are then supposed to generate the visible world in all its multifarious appearances. They are also supposed eternally to produce peace, harmony, even unity; but because the model is sexual and generative they never do; instead, they produce new division in the form of children, and unity is further off than ever:

A father, mother, child, a daughter or a son,
That's how all natural or supernatural stories run.

(Yeats, 'Supernatural Songs,' II)

There's no disputing the immense power the mind has attained by its characteristic grammatical device of dividing all things into two; it is in that way that it rules. Language, made of warring opposites, becomes the instrument of conquest and domination, which may be why the mind is so marvelous at dealing with things and so foolish or so wicked at applying the same instrument to human beings. And not the least interesting of the many paradoxes that attach to this theme is that this great linguistic power of abstracting, essentializing, simplifying, and making the whole visible world over in the image of two warring armies (form and matter, for example) goes hand in hand with, and even succeeds by, the most delicate, devoted, even loving observation of particulars. Language and the eye again relate.

Consider this power of language. A mathematician (Kronecker) said, 'God made the integers, man did the rest.' Might we not consent to a similar mythical origin for the alphabet (no matter what we think we know of the history of the matter)? For here is the human ingenium going forth into the world with its three dozen bits and pieces of stuff such as never was on land or sea, and addressing the mute phenomena with its silly-looking battle cries of 1, 2, 3 ... and A, B, C.... Whereupon, to take a swift overview of the process, the dumb creation wakened and began to produce epic poetry, codes of law, astronomy, arts of agriculture and of warfare, and the earth opened and put forth the strange blossoms and fruits of TV sets, refrigerators, Cadillacs, and electronic computers that can put a million things in order before you can say 1, 2, 3.... It is at any rate astounding to contemplate, and whether or no it is edifying we have little enough else to be edified by.

Now what I am wondering is whether there may not be some means of getting past this contradiction in our natures of which language is the expression. (I was about to say 'of overcoming this contradiction,' but that is again a figure from warfare, such as comes all too easily to mind in the present world, so that even pacifists speak hopefully of 'an all-out assault on war.') For doesn't it seem as though the mind, in adapting language as the mode of its activity, settled too soon and too easily for too little? Even the poets, I suspect, are getting tired of this perpetual fiddling with opposites, which is what abstract and speculative thought produces, and all it produces, when it is not producing television sets on whose screens two cowboys or two astronauts or two housewives will represent opposite points of view. Isn't there something else?

And again, of course, echo answers. I don't know, and the mere thought of that 'something else' may be but another form of the delusion whereby human beings seek to escape from the hard conditions of life in the world. But if I can't answer, I can at least give an instance of how the mind in opting for language as its model, and preferring that instrument over seeing, may have diminished itself in comparison of what was possible.

A man recognizes his friend and says hello. In a time immeasurably brief, with no evident intervention of thought, immensely delicate discriminations have been carried out with complete success. On the unpromising ground of a generalized architectural similarity—two eyes, a nose, a mouth, and so on—the exact pattern of one among an indefinitely large number of variations has locked itself into place with a solidity admitting of no doubt whatever. Now, for contrast, imagine the man trying to describe his friend to a stranger in such a way as to bring about, even if not instantaneously, the same recognition: instead of absolute precision there will now be vagueness, instead of the richness of recognition there will now be the poverty of language—and paradoxically, at the same time, the whole ensemble of features in characteristic motion, the whole fugue of expression, will have been unbearably simplified and over-specified, not to mention that it will have its action stopped as by a photograph—but more radically than by a photograph, more like asking someone to recognize a musical composition by playing one not very distinctive chord that occurs in it. 'He has brown eyes and wavy hair.' By language, then, the world is simplified and specified in the interest of a supposed exactness, but the simplicity and specificity turn out to be, by comparison with experience, largely illusory, productive of helpless generality and ill-fitting mythology.

And yet this miraculously delicate and strong power of recognition is in us, no less than conscious intellection is in us. I mean to ask: Could language somehow be persuaded to come closer to experience? I think that to a small extent it sometimes happens in poetry. And I think that Joyce, in *Finnegans Wake,* meant so to extend the range of mind by getting it, so to say, down out of the head, where it seemed finally to have taken up its abode. For ever so much of *Finnegans Wake*—and ever so much of its difficulty for the reader lies in this rather than in any question of knowledge—is an attempt to represent the actual, rather than the ideally or conventionally rational, occurrence of thought in language by showing how bodily a thing language really is, and the grand geniality of the work has much to do with the comedy of the rational intelligence trying to speak its sensible but thin evidences while the unconscious is twisting and translating and garbling its words and the body is keeping up a huge cacophony—or is it really a symphony?—of grunts and snores and farts and belches and coughs, and the ancestral dead, most of them drunk, are also getting in on the act with their accumulated wisdom and their accumulated nonsense, all of which, if we will have it, is ours.

In conclusion, I acknowledge gratefully that it is only the existence of language as a model for thought that has made it possible for me to discuss the inadequacies of language as a model for thought; and if I have said anything against language, I sincerely apologize.

ON POETRY AND PAINTING, WITH A THOUGHT OF MUSIC

⸙ ᒣᘐᕊ ⸙

There are affinities between poetry and painting, and perhaps the words 'image' and 'language' will help focus these as well as the differences. Painters make images, poets make images; the painter too has language, though not perhaps in so explicit a sense as the poet does; the palette for a given landscape, say, acts as a negative kind of syntax, excluding certain colors from the range of possibility; and as a positive kind as well, indicating the possibilities of gradation in getting from earth through river through forest to sky.

Both poet and painter want to reach the silence behind the language, the silence within the language. Both painter and poet want their work to shine not only in daylight but (by whatever illusionist magic) from within; maybe even more from within than by daylight, for many of their works in times now past had not the object of being viewed in daylight but went to do their magic in caves, in tombs, among the dead, and maybe as a substitute for daylight.

The poet walks through the museum and among so many and so diverse conceptions and manners of treatment he sees, he hears, especially two things: silence and light. Viewing the picture frames as windows, he looks into rooms, out of rooms into landscapes—what the Chinese call 'mountain-water pictures'—and knows from the silence that he is seeing the past, the dead, the irrevocable; and he knows something else, that what he sees is not only the past, the dead, the irrevocable, but something that had the intention of being these things from the moment of its conception: something that is, so to say, past from the beginning. Hence the great silence common among so many differences of subject and execution; hence, too, the solemnity of the museum, crowded with solitudes; the dignity of painting, that stands in a sort of enchanted space between life and death.

He sees also that the light in these rectangles appears to come from within. In the work of an unknown master he sees the thin veil of a small waterfall in sunlight—amazing! He leans in to look closer, the threads of water become white paint mixed with a little gray on a gray ground—amazing again, not quite in the same way, that crossing-point, that exact distance, within which illusion becomes paint, beyond which paint becomes illusion again. Whereas in the painting of a river by Vlaminck, the thin, pale surface of the water, bearing the thinnest and most shivering of pale reflections, is made by means of the heaviest, thickest, grossest applications of paint, made with a virtuosity that is able to make colored dirt produce effects of light. Amazing again.

His own art, in the comparison, begins to seem the merest pitifullest chatter, compounded of impatience and opinion. On thoughts like this, the poet finds it best to hasten from the museum, that marvelous tomb-temple wherein the living are privileged to look so deeply into what is no more, experiencing their own mortality as a dignified silence not without its effects of grandeur and austerity; though all this *looking deeply,* that so magicks the beholder, is done on a plane surface.

Out in the day again, he thinks about the matter some more. First about some poems of his own time, especially some he cares for, that have a relation with painting or drawing. There is Auden's 'Musée des Beaux Arts,' with its reflections that rely on Brueghel, on *The Fall of Icarus* and on the *Massacre of the Innocents.* There is John Berryman's 'Hunters Returning at Evening,' also referring to Brueghel; there is Randall Jarrell's emblem drawn from Dürer's *Knight, Death, and Devil;* there is even one of his own, composed and called after René Magritte's *The Human Condition (I).* These things have a relation to painting, and they are not painting. It would be interesting to speculate what that relation might be.

It is not, certainly, that the poems speak about the paintings they refer to; no, for the poems offer relatively bare and selective descriptions; no art student sent to the museum would dare come back with such descriptions, which sometimes hardly serve to identify the paintings. No, the poems speak about the silence of the paintings; and where the poet was lucky his poem will speak the silence of the painting; it too will say nothing more than: It is so, it is as it is. The poem, too, when it works, is a concentrated shape illuminated by an energy from within; its opinions do not matter, but it matters. Here, too, he observes, all that happens happens while the poem, like the painting, lies flat on a plane surface, the surface of the page.

From the other side, he is reassured to think, ever so much of painting comes from poetry, refers to poetry, and is poetical in its own nature as well as in its subject matter. Not only the biblical subjects, for example, but the various conceptions and styles that transfigure the subjects, that poetize upon the Crucifixion, say, with respect to an eternal glory in so many medieval masters, a superhuman grandeur in Michelangelo, a bitter suffering in Grünewald, the light of an ordinary day in Brueghel.

So both painter and poet are makers of images, and traditionally there is a connection between the images they make. And when we say they *make* images, we do not seek to distinguish, for the present, the component of invention from that of discovery.

And both painter and poet write in languages. This seems at first to mark a decisive and unbridgeable difference, the difference in their languages. But it invites a little further thought.

Surely the painter's language has the dignity of being the oldest ever written down. Minerals, plants, the liquids of the body even to blood, all gave up their substance many thousand years ago to the representation by signs of perceptions based upon fear, desire, hunger, dreams, and a certain decorative and geometrizing distance from all these, a certain coldness. Whereas writing came much later. Writing in an alphabet wholly independent of pictorial elements is usually dated not much earlier than the middle of the second millennium B.C.

Perhaps nothing in the alphabet cannot also be seen in nature: O in a hole, W or M in a distant flying bird, Y in the branching of a tree, and so on. But that's not pertinent. What really matters is that no alphabet could exist as long as these signs were seen exclusively as belonging to nature; they had to be got out of nature, so that you could write C without any thought of the curve of the shoreline, S without thinking about snakes, any letter without thinking of it except as a letter— something that had never before been, something in effect literally 'nonsensical' that yet could 'make sense' of the realms to which its immense range of combinations was applied. If the conservative element in society got as mithered as it did at the advent of 'abstract art' at the Armory Show of 1913, imagine its probable resentment at so great an innovation as the alphabet: 'It don't look like anything I ever seen,' 'A child could do stuff like that if he thought it worth the bother,' and so on.

With respect to painting, E. H. Gombrich, who has written so beautifully against the grain of an abstract age about the miraculous thing that is representation, suggests that perhaps painting too arose out of coincidences in nature—as the alphabet did, but in the opposite direction. The earliest cave drawings might have been, he speculates, those in which a peculiar form of the rock itself was first *recognized* as resembling an animal, and then modified by artistic means with a view to increasing the degree of this resemblance; rather as the earliest portrait statuary, too, employed the human skull itself as armature—a thought that even yet retains a depth of sinister magical intent.

And the development of painting might be conceived of as having three main branches. The first would be in the direction of greater fidelity to appearances, ending in the peculiar magic of the waxworks, which so clearly and instantly distinguishes itself from the magic of art. The second would be in the direction of ornament, rhythm, pattern, figuration, of an abstract character. And the third would be in the direction of language, of alphabet and the codifying of signs, ending in the magic of writing; the process is indeed perceptible in the history of Chinese writing; while in Egypt, though writing and painting were clearly distinguishable, yet writing remained a species of representational drawing, though abstract and conditioned by the introduction of specifically linguistic and nonrepresentational signs.

It will be worthwhile to remember here Coomaraswamy's (Ananda Kentish Coomaraswamy, *Christian and Oriental Philosophy of Art* [New York: Dover, 1956], passim) demonstration that in traditions of sacred art, the medieval Christian as much as the Hindu, painting was treated as linguistic; the characters of iconography were dictated at least as much by the codified formulas of priesthoods as by any free observation of the visible world; which offers an answer, and a good one, to the question of how, in a world without photography, the features of gods and saviors become so quickly fixed and invariant.

In both languages, then, of writing and of painting, the shapes and substances of the earth rose up and assumed a mental and a spiritual quality, conferring upon the mind that brought them forth a thrilling if somewhat frightening power of detachment from the world as viewed by the prehuman mind, or at least the mind that was before these things were.

Maybe the comparison has to end there. For push and pull as we may, writing and painting *did* separate off from one another. Might they ever come back together? Ought they ever to come back together? If their very different but immense powers were to fuse into something not really much like either—what then?

We do already have an instance in which this happens: the making of maps, charts, diagrams, blueprints . . . where the representing of the visible, at which painting is supremely capable, is accomplished in parallel with the strict and abstract syntax of writing able without modification of its own nature to transmit an indefinite variety of messages, which is the supreme contribution of written language. Might this somewhat elementary compound of writing and painting have still some way to go in the world?

I should like to make a rather wild leap at such a question, and hope to be going in a forward direction. Writing and painting could come together, though I don't know in the least what their offspring would look like. (Possibly it would not *look* at all.) It is here that I get the vaguest glimmer of a hint from music, or from some thoughts about music. Proust touches the thought, but almost at once lets it go:

> And just as certain creatures are the last surviving testimony to a form of life which nature has discarded, I asked myself if music were not the unique example of what might have been—if there had not come the invention of language, the formation of words, the analysis of ideas—the means of communication between one spirit and another. It is like a possibility which has ended in nothing.
>
> (Marcel Proust, *The Remembrance of Things Past,* translated by C. K. Scott-Moncrieff [New York: Random House, 1934], II, 560)

Another writer, François le Lionnais (*The Orion Book of Time,* translated by William D. O'Gorman, Jr. [New York: The Orion Press, 1966], p. 108), also encourages this sort of speculation, also without demonstration, when he says that certain music—his examples are the Elizabethan virginalists, J. S. Bach, Schumann, Anton von Webern—'consists not only of fluctuating sound patterns capable of delighting the ear but also of psychological hieroglyphics not yet decoded.'

The vaguest glimmer of a hint, and one which I am, at least at present, unable to take any further, though perhaps some of my readers may. For this of 'hieroglyphics' and 'decoding' has its charms, because the arts have always had, in addition to their popular side, their deep affinity for mystery and the esoteric, for the secret which is also the sacred.

SPEAKING SILENCE

The question of the relation between poetry and meaning—what has it traditionally been? has it been changing? how to describe it at present?—is a poignantly appropriate one to address to teachers of English, because the teacher of English makes his modest but respectable living out of the presumption that such a relation helpfully exists and is readily visible in the course of reading particular poems with his pupils, even if the relation in general is far from clear. If, on the one hand, this relation should at all largely cease to be effective, the teacher would be out of a job. But if the relation should become easy and obvious to the dullest student, the teacher would also be out of a job. There is a real danger in teaching too well; that in time the lesson will actually be absorbed. Not that we often feel this danger to be imminent, and yet in some sense that is what seems to have happened with respect to the teaching of certain sorts of explicative criticism, which in twenty or thirty years reduced poems of formidable difficulty and formidable glamor to freshman and even high school senior exercises; familiarity breeding what it is proverbially said to do. Concerning this, I allow myself one remark based on a couple of dozen years at teaching: the world has got no wiser, but it has got a great deal smarter. Or, paraphrasing Yeats, things taught too long can be no longer taught.

No doubt that is in some part a good thing. It reassuringly suggests that lessons do get learned, and, even more mysteriously, that lessons learned by trained minds do become, by a sort of intellectual osmosis, available to younger and less-trained minds; become in some sense the *habitus* of all even moderately literate minds, a part of the intellectual weather. At least, that is the optimistic way of putting it. But there is a less happy aspect, and it is this: to be taught, and to be learned, the lesson must be intellectualized; accordingly what is learned, the pessimist might argue, is not at all a *habitus* of mind or a style of thought, but only a few cheap tricks, glib remarks, and the habit of dropping famous names. For truly, as Owen Barfield says, there is a spirit in the world, in the mind of the world, who freezes: 'His purpose is to destroy everything in human thinking which depends on a certain warmth, to replace wonder by sophistication, courtesy by vulgarity, understanding by calculation, imagination by statistics' (*Unancestral Voice* [Middletown, Connecticut: Wesleyan University Press, 1965], p. 59). In that thoughtfully selected set of antitheses I hope to find my subject. For the working of that cold spirit, whom Mr. Barfield calls Ahriman after the Persian god of darkness, is visible in a number of ways that affect us professionally as well as personally: in an ever more confirmedly angry and nihilistic posture of the literary mind; in a dry and overly rationalist style of teaching that emphasizes answers at the expense of questions; and perhaps especially in this, that in an important sense our teaching seems not to work. That is, it ought to be a major object of English studies to make available to the student a large number of works, together with a way of looking at them and the world, that will go with him through his life, as companionable guides, as friendly masters, as austere instructors, as charitable consolers. Now so far as I am able to see this does not happen. Of the millions of schoolchildren, and the hundreds of thousands of young men and women in the colleges, or at any rate of my small sampling from these categories, a great many are vitally, even fiercely, interested in literature, and pursue it even to the exclusion of more practical-appearing and materially rewarding studies. But to the degree that one is able to look at life outside the academy—the life of these same young people later on—our efforts seem bound to appear as having been of null or negligible effect. A very few become writers, and a much larger number enters the teaching profession. But such evidence as has become available to me suggests that as a rule those graduates who do not concern themselves with literature in some professional capacity do not concern themselves with literature at all.

But here I must pause for a few words of caution, as much to myself as to you. First, what I say on this point may simply not be true. I have made no surveys, collected no statistics, but rely on impressions from travel, conversation, and reading. Second, if it is true, as I assume it is, it is not necessary to suppose the fault to lie with ourselves and the conduct of our classes. The world outside is a sufficiently grim, dull, grinding, and demanding place, which may well require of the candidate for success therein that he jettison a good deal of meditative and imaginative baggage.

Even if I proceed, as I am going to, on the assumptions that I have described the situation as it is and that a substantial part of the blame lies with our teaching, I am forced to face a third objection. The last thing a teacher is likely to know about, as a general subject, is teaching. He rarely—there are exceptions—gets to see his colleagues at work, and has never got enough evidence to make possible a generalization from their procedures; and as for his own procedures, he has scarcely any view of them at all, because when he teaches he is too busy teaching to be able to stand back and watch himself doing it. So what I shall say about the practices of a hypothetical, Platonic archetype of an English teacher is at the best mythological, speculative, founded on nothing more evidentially impressive than rumor and introspection. In the interests of a kind of literary perfectionism, moreover, I shall try to make our professional lives out to be not merely difficult but impossible, before asking myself if there is any remedy. Henry Adams convinced himself by the end of his first year on the Harvard faculty that teaching is of its nature an impossibility; and we have also the word of William James, in a conversation by chance preserved, that 'the natural enemy of any subject is the professor thereof.' And surely we will many times have resembled, to our students, that monster in an old movie of whom Hope said to Crosby, 'Sure it doesn't have any teeth. But it could gum you to death.'

So. I shall be delighted if, after this paper, some of you can set my ignorance straight and tell me flatly that there is nothing wrong, nothing at all wrong, and that we are all, in our classrooms, models of intellectual virtue and imaginative charity . . . delighted. But maybe also a touch surprised. On this, two small anecdotes.

I once worked at a college whose trustees were very high on faculty self-criticism, examination of conscience, and so on. Every year they would send to each department a questionnaire whose tendency was to the effect of: 'Are you sure you are doing the right thing? are you sure you are doing it as well as possible?' A sort of Chinese communist, or Jesuitical, view of life. But the chairman of the department used to reply, year in and year out, and without bothering to circulate the questionnaire, 'The department is doing its work with the usual absolute distinction. After prolonged and concentrated reflection we find our operations to be superb.' This formidable reassurance was never, as far as I know, questioned by anyone.

Second anecdote. A teacher and writer to whom I owe a good deal (Kenneth Burke) was at dinner with a teacher and writer to whom he professed to owe a good deal (I. A. Richards). At the end of the glorious evening, the old man, putting on his overshoes, said to the very old man, 'I love you and admire you, but tell me, where did we go wrong?' And the very old man looked kindly at the old man and said with great gentleness, 'We didn't go wrong.'

And so to business.

Most simply, the purpose of this paper is to outline, with respect to poetry, a species of teaching somewhat different from the one we usually employ. I am not trying to overthrow one method and substitute another, only to suggest that there really are two methods, which properly complement one another, and that our standard practice in teaching is to use the one almost exclusively and neglect the other.

The method I suspect we all use exclusively, or almost so, may be called analytic, and has to do broadly with finding out the meanings of poems; if one wanted to be critical of that method one could call it, as a friend of mine did, 'how to turn poems into prose,' with the subtitle: 'look how sensitive I am.'

The method I am going to propose as the complement to the first is both simple and difficult, though I hope not impossible. It has to do less with 'teaching poetry' than with 'being taught by poetry.' Its presumptions are these. First, that though poets may not think, their poems do. Second, and it may be the same thing from another angle, a poem is not so much a thought, or series of thoughts, as it is a mind. No doubt it is a much-simplified mind, in comparison of the only other sort we know. And yet, in the presence of an attentive human mind a poem will recognizably think; sometimes it will think thoughts that are deep and strange indeed.

In short, given that poetry is a language, our way of showing pupils how to deal with it is to translate out of that language into our own more familiar one. Suppose, however, another object, the one we ordinarily have in studying any language: to learn to speak it, and at last to learn to think in it. This figurative way of putting the matter—but I am not at all sure it is entirely figurative—tells me that I may be wrong in thinking of the two ways as opposites; rather, in experience, one ought to follow the other. Then my complaint about our teaching would be that we never get, nor induce our students to get, from the first way to the second, from translating out of the poetic language to thinking in it.

It is not hard to see why we teach as we do, analytically; and seeing to sympathize with our plight. For the teacher, as Ezra Pound tersely defined him, is a man who must talk for an hour. It is a good definition, for even if it be not the whole truth it is an aspect of the truth that for dignity's sake we frequently suppress, even to ourselves. It is a simple definition to appearance, and yet heavy with consequences.

For if you have to talk for an hour, you concentrate naturally enough on what is sayable, you stress those elements in the object before you which are most amenable to translation, paraphrase, commentary; and as far as it goes that's fair. But it doesn't go far enough, and in certain respects it may be harmful to your relation with the object. For it may imply—despite the usual disclaimers—that you exhaust the object's interest by making explicit everything possible about it. Also, with whatever goodwill, you are substituting for the object the number of things, sometimes a large number of things, possible to be said about it.

In practice, another consequence follows. We tend to teach, at least I know I tend to teach, poems I think I more or less understand, at least in an intellectual sense; and these poems will be chiefly in a middle range, neither those that are simplest in appearance nor those that are appallingly difficult will often become the object of teaching. Blake's 'The Clod & the Pebble' will stand for an instance of the first; Hart Crane's 'At Melville's Tomb' for an instance of the second (and I have taught them, but with the help of my second method).

Still another consequence. Owing to the difficulties already mentioned, we find ourselves concentrating on poems that exemplify certain sorts of intellectual difficulty that demand explanation; for the teacher, not unnaturally, loveth best what teachest best.

The claim I make in the foregoing may be summed up so. The art work is silent, we must speak. The beautiful is a category of experience by itself, it is *sui generis,* it does not really translate into something else even though it may seem to do so at certain points—because poetry employs a language full of words that are also used for other than poetic purposes.

I shall now present an example, a poem by Herbert, and use it to describe two sorts of teaching, the one we usually do and the other one that I am proposing, not as a substitute for the first, but as appropriate in two ways, as a prelude to interpretation and then, much later, as the fulfillment of interpretation.

Prayer, the Churches banquet, Angels age,
  Gods breath in man returning to his birth,
  The soul in paraphrase, heart in pilgrimage,
The Christian plummet sounding heav'n and earth;

Engine against th'Almighty, sinner's towre,
  Reversed thunder, Christ-side-piercing spear,
  The six-daies-world transposing in an houre,
A kinde of tune, which all things heare and fear;

Softnesse, and peace, and joy, and love, and blisse,
  Exalted Manna, gladnesse of the best,
  Heaven in ordinarie, man well drest,
The milkie way, the bird of Paradise,
  Church-bels beyond the stars heard, the souls blood,
  The land of spices, something understood.

('Prayer')

With this poem by George Herbert there is much that the analyzing reason may properly do. We see that it is a sonnet, we see that it is entirely composed of definitions, or names, for prayer, which may or may not be synonymous with one another, and that these names or definitions are all of them metaphorical. Going a little further, we see that the language of the poem is the language of a man to whom the Bible is second nature, and it may be helpful to ourselves as well as to our pupils to refer back to the source of some of his expressions: the plummet, the spear, the six-days-world, manna; even man well drest, which comes from the parable of the Gadarene swine (Mark v.15: And they come to Jesus, and see him that was possessed with the devil, and had the legion, sitting, and clothed, and in his right mind), though it means also that one goes to church in one's best clothes.

And probably, by the application of this same analytical intelligence, we could go a great deal further and do a great many more things. We could discuss, as anthologies of a critical sort tell us to do, theme, attitude, tone, rhythm, meter . . . and after discussing these and other high matters, such as that not all these expressions go the same way: some are homely, others exotic; some are reverent, others audacious to the point of almost blasphemy—that Christ-side-piercing spear is rather a shocker—after all this we could come up with some sort of result in the form of a summary. The poem says . . . the poem is. . . . And all this will have been useful work; I do not in the least mean to sneer at analysis, critical thinking, learning. . . . It will have been useful work, except—except that in a way it seems not to have an object. Santayana defined confusion as redoubling your efforts when you have lost sight of the goal, and I have a sense that something like this is what happens if our discussion of the poem, however accurate and thoughtful, leaves off where it is.

For there is something we have not touched on, and probably, though we do not say so aloud, we believe our methods forbid us from doing so. It is the strangeness of it all. And in strangeness there is beauty, there is access to beauty.

Or maybe you don't feel it as strange—the poem itself, the situation of teacher and pupils reading and talking about the poem? It is not strange, perhaps, only because, if I have made a fair though summary representation of it, it's just what we do all the time. So I shall try to unpack and spread out a little of what is in this word 'strangeness.'

Much of education proceeds, and rightly, by making the strange familiar, interpreting the unknown in terms of the known, and so on, which is more or less what we mean by explaining something. For example, the word 'current' in discussions of electricity seems to tell us that the invisible and strange was named from the visible and familiar, from current in water. And probably a beginning of explanation could profitably take this into account.

But I wish us now to consider the opposite process, and suggest that a part of teaching ought to consist in making the familiar strange. That at least would be the normal way of saying it, but as often happens the normal way of saying it is wrong, being not strange enough itself. Rather than 'making the familiar strange,' which suggests strangeness appliquéd onto familiar substance, I shall say 'revealing the strangeness that is already there.'

Put it this way. On the one side is the teacher, quite familiar (let us assume) with the poem, the relevant learning that fits him to deal with the poem, with George Herbert's poetry in general, with the seventeenth century and the quality of its diction, and so on. On the other side is the pupil, to whom the poem (let us assume, again) is not so much strange as it is odd, perhaps disagreeably so: it is about a subject he doesn't much care for and which seems to him to need no discussion; it is confused, for if prayer is one of these things how can it be another, or all the others; it is written in a language he partly doesn't understand, but what he does understand is not any better for it bores him stiff and seems queasily sentimental besides—all that about softness and peace and joy and love and bliss makes him squirm slightly.

Now which of the two, pupil or teacher, is at the greater disadvantage with the poem? I'm not sure I can decide myself, but I am convinced the answer would not be unequivocally in the teacher's favor. Both teacher and pupil will have to see the object with new eyes before the learning of the one can be relevant or the ignorance of the other be remedied.

But how can this be done? Isn't this a dead end? One of those things which just is or isn't? Well, I think it can in part be done, though not easily, and only by proceeding in a rather strange fashion. For all the way to strangeness is strange. What I am proposing may be but the Socratic method reversed, moving toward ignorance instead of toward knowledge. Or, to put it as a slogan: before studying atoms, study void. And I should warn you, that this sort of teaching requires as much silence as talk, or maybe a bit more. As teachers, I fear, we are professionally afraid of silence in the classroom, because it usually means incompetence. But of course there is another sort, summed up in a taoist maxim which shrewdly hits us where we make our living: the sages are silent, the talented talk, the fools argue. A remark of that sort surely makes my situation a trifle peculiar at this moment, standing up here flapping my mouth in favor of silence. But then, it would be no bad definition of the art work itself to say of it that it was a speaking silence, or of poetry that it is a means of seeing invisible things and saying unspeakable things about them.

Suppose—and now I will make an example of my own procedures—suppose that instead of beginning with explanations we begin with the refusal to explain. There are several epithets in the poem that strike me as difficult in such a way that they do not yield to explanation very readily, and may not do so at all. Possibly 'the soul in paraphrase' cannot be paraphrased. Certainly it will not be clarified by more information about, or definitions of, either soul or paraphrase. We all know, more or less, or assume we do until this moment when we inspect the matter more closely, what soul means and what paraphrase means; only we don't know what 'soul in paraphrase' means. Similarly, we know reversed and we know thunder, but 'reversed thunder' is another thing entirely.

I don't mean to exaggerate. Probably we could fudge up more or less satisfactory explanations of these figures. But the object of this exercise is precisely not to do that.

Suppose instead we ask our students to think the phrase 'reversed thunder' in connection with prayer for, say, two minutes. No doubt this is dangerous, for if some of the students disobeyed we should have no means of knowing it. Still, suppose we try. And we caution the students that they are not to think *about* the expression 'reversed thunder,' they are to think it.

Now I submit that when this is done, something, not nothing, begins to happen, though we are hardly yet at the point where what happens becomes a question on the final exam; indeed, we may never get there. But what is this something?

I think it is this. There is first a sense of sinking in upon the phrase. You are meditating it, you are not meditating about it. There comes then, I believe, a somewhat fearful sense that might be called an apprehension of insanity, though not perhaps a very serious one—for you could stop at any time—but I should rather call it a general and surprising apprehension of the precariousness of all language, meaning, knowledge. And then, perhaps, if the meditation is prolonged a bit further, a third thing happens: the expression 'reversed thunder' becomes an unmediated name for prayer, a name that one will henceforth apply on fit occasion as unhesitatingly and unquestioningly as one applies the name 'elm' to a particular tree. This will have happened, if it does, in the first place because a poet did something profoundly right in language; in the second place, because you responded to his language by using it as it was meant to be used: by listening to it and making it your own rather than by quickly translating it into something else rather like it.

Now this may be silly; certainly it will feel silly at first. But before trying to meet objections, I want to carry my description of this procedure a bit further.

I suggested we should begin with the hardest phrases in the poem, because when we go at it this way they become paradoxically the easiest and most obvious ones. For if you are moving toward ignorance instead of toward knowledge, everything else will be turned round too. Other such phrases, in this poem, are 'the soul in paraphrase,' and 'the six-daies-world transposing in an houre.' With 'reversed thunder' they share the characteristic that we know right away we do not understand them. In their turn, subjected to a meditation emptied of thoughts *about* them, they may become names, in every respect equivalent to the ordinary names for things that we learned as children, so that they now seem irrevocably right. Or they may not. The thing may not happen every time, and the reason why not may be located anywhere between George Herbert and ourselves; it doesn't seem important to decide. Poets are not equally fine at every moment, and neither are readers.

Now the next stage. We chose those phrases because they were hard to understand; well, fresh from the perception of what happened with them, let us try returning to phrases we believed we understood at once. Applying the same meditation to these, to 'Exalted Manna,' for instance, or to 'a kinde of tune, which all things heare and fear,' we shall find, I believe, that our idea of understanding shakes down only to this, that we felt able to express the same idea in different words. I fancy that our new and close way of looking will in certain instances convince ourselves of having been merely mistaken, for 'Angels age' now looks much harder than it did. But even where we are able to paraphrase as we think correctly, we shall attain to at least the second of the three stages described above: the general and surprising apprehension of the precariousness of all language, meaning, knowledge . . . and it may be that certain profound stirrings, vague recognitions and acknowledgments, a little bit exciting and also a little bit frightening, will begin to arise in the minds of pupils and teachers carrying out this contemplation. What these are may be better shadowed forth than said out loud and clear, but the beginning of them is plain enough, it will be a lively sense of the strangeness of the language that gives us the human world, the world of thought and feeling, and that may at any moment deprive us of the same. It will lead us to look with wonder upon the emergence of meaning out of things, and upon the sinking of meaning into things which is the product of human artifice. For the organization of inert bits of matter into a television set is just as much a product of language as the poem by George Herbert which we have kept so long before us.

I must not leave it, however, without taking at least one further step. The poem ends with what may well be the simplest expression of all, having a grave sweetness, kindness, and a finality of its own appropriate to its position: 'something understood.' It seems to me as though, after such meditations in silence as I have tried to describe, we might now be in a position to do some useful talking. Herbert's genius in ending the poem thus seems to me a matter for deeper wonder the more I look at it, suggesting that what we call genius is but the capacity for being absolutely relevant. The little phrase is indeed an epiphany, and maybe now we have been prepared to receive it.

For the thoughts evoked in us by our meditation on certain of the poet's phrases were not so much about prayer as they were about thought, meaning, understanding, language in general; and now the simple and reflexive 'something understood' shows us greater mysteries than all the complexities and difficulties and plain oddities that we considered before, only we could not properly come to this one without considering first those others. But now we see that the overt subject, prayer, is a high and mysterious analogy for something much more everyday but equally mysterious and equally miraculous: prayer is an analogue for language generally, and for the strangest thing of all, that sometimes when we speak we are understood, sometimes when others speak we understand, and when this happens our recognition of the fact that it has happened is simple and silent; at most we say, 'yes, I see.' Yet what has happened is, if we inspect it in full consciousness, a great happiness, for where perplexity was there is now harmony and agreement. And when this happens, even in the least and most trivial instance, a miraculous thing has happened: language has produced silence, and the talented touch on the realm where the sages live. Formally, one might add, after following the whole course of the poet's thought, that all the other expressions are now meant to be rejected; they were necessary, but only as a way of reaching 'something understood,' which by the paradox of strangeness could not have been understood at all had it appeared alone or come first instead of last.

What I have been trying to describe is the first couple of steps on a road that may go further and may not; also it may lead somewhere worth going and it may not. I've been hardly a couple of steps further myself than I have so far tried to take you, so I don't know. No doubt there are many objections to what I have said, and perhaps I should try to anticipate one or two of the most powerful of those.

The one I should most immediately expect is that all this about silence and meditation, about 'sinking in upon phrases,' and so on, is, or at least very quickly leads to, the most arrant mystery-fakery, laziness, intellectual self-indulgence, and that the teacher who tries it will merely be infecting his pupils with these undesirable traits. I feel rather keenly, myself, that something like that could well be the case, though it needn't be. In that sense, perhaps such a word as 'meditation' has too queer a sound, and ought not to be used. Nor should anything in the line of a religiose solemnity be associated with the procedure I outlined. For, as I hope I have made plain at several points already, I am not against reasoned criticism, scholarship, or what might be called the ordinary processes of thought if experience didn't tell us how extraordinary they are, at all; it is only that the silent kind of contemplation of the object I propose is necessary in the first place if our thoughts are to find something to think about, and in the last place if our thoughts are to find some kind of fulfillment, some kind of completion, appropriate to the object.

An even more powerful objection would be that even if I reached an appropriate response to Herbert's poem at last, all that about the silent inspection of its bits and pieces was largely irrelevant decor; that when I finally came to grips with the piece I did it in the ordinary manner, by reasoning as hard as I could about it. To this I should say that I don't think so, but that it is a point on which it is very easy to be deceived. For one thing, I had to write out the process, and that seems to me a good bit harder than doing it in class. But I did, in writing it out, actually follow the process I described, and the results that turned up appeared to me as both surprising and just. Again I would say to this objection that I am not advocating the substitution of something else for thinking, but only a kind of deep sensing that provides the materials for thinking to work on, as it will also provide, later on, the satisfaction of such thinking as we may be able to do. In this connection I would remind you of the paradoxical situation I alluded to at the beginning: that the success of explicative criticism is exactly its failure. The more easily our sharper pupils handle the critical apparatus given them to play with—the jungle gyms and Skinner boxes arranged by systematic criticism—the more, and the more justly, we feel that they are doing something perfunctory and only superficially intelligent, something they can do precisely because it comes nowhere near them. We had the experience, but we missed the meaning, said Mr. Eliot. But it would be true to say about a vast lot of what goes on in the curriculum of the English department, that we had the meaning but missed the experience.

But now, instead of trying to state and meet further objections, I shall revert to some of the thoughts behind what I have said so far, and say a bit also about where they appear to lead.

To begin with, I raised the question of the relation between poetry and meaning, and asked if possibly that relation had not been changing rather radically during the past while. I suggested that the kind of 'close reading' I, along with many of you, had been brought up to do, the kind identified in its beginnings with such critics as Richards, Empson, Burke, Brooks, and Warren, and later, around 1940, labeled (by Ransom) The New Criticism, had run its course. In a sense it seemed to have taught its lesson all too successfully, so that 'meanings' could be extracted from poems faster and more efficiently, by its mechanisms, than ever before . . . until at last no one, and especially not the student, was any longer interested in these meanings or in the process of their extraction.

Then I went right away from this frightening topic to speak of a possible other way of dealing with poems, though this other way, when at last I produced it, was far from revolutionary, inasmuch as it didn't in the least mean to overthrow interpretation but only to restore to it a certain reality which had been lost. This other way seemed bent on stressing not the explicability of poems but far rather their mysterious otherness which resisted explanations; and behind my discussion of the example from Herbert appeared this theme: poetic language as the way in which meaning gets into the world, or (without prejudice) the way in which meaning is made to arise out of the world. And I spoke for a moment, rather darkly, about how language, that confers thought and feeling upon the world, may turn upon itself and deprive us and the world of thought and feeling. On this theme I have, by way of conclusion, a very few things to say, which may rightly be introduced by repeating Owen Barfield's characterization of a spirit in the world whose purpose is 'to destroy everything in human thinking which depends on a certain warmth, to replace wonder by sophistication, courtesy by vulgarity, understanding by calculation, imagination by statistics.'

Here is an impossible exercise. Try to imagine in a few moments the entire course of English Literature, our professional domain, with the study of it and the means to that study, since English became recognizably the language it is, about six centuries ago. Try to reflect on the succession of its appearances in time. To make the task a little easier, I shall limit the subject to the greatest works, and only those in poetry.

Naming off the highest peaks in the range, the permanently visible: Chaucer and Langland, Spenser, Shakespeare, Milton, Pope, Blake, Wordsworth. . . . Now I call your attention to a little fog forming in the valleys, the first hint of it in late Tudor times; fog, mist, cloud . . . for if I start with mountain ranges I must follow the figure . . . and the names of these are scholarship, apparatus, editions, criticism, biography, bibliography. The moment Elizabeth dies, bang! comes the first English dictionary.

I drop the metaphor just as the clouds begin to conceal the mountain peaks themselves, about a hundred years ago when English first became a subject of study in college and universities; English departments came even after that. For I don't believe that learning and its necessary instruments are really fog, mist, cloud. And indeed, I am not criticizing, or suggesting that you criticize, what happened; I am only holding it up so that we can see what happened.

Looking at the latter part of this time-lapse film, taking it from 1800, say, I submit that what we see, and see, in so rapid an overview, overwhelmingly and to the exclusion of much else, is an accelerating production of language about language, and that this accelerating production also accelerates the rate of its acceleration. I suggest, too, that more and more of this language about other language comes under the head of explaining things. I chose the expression 'language about language' as the most general and inclusive term that will cover what is common to criticism, biography, bibliography, the making of dictionaries, concordances, glossaries, variorum editions, histories of literature... explorations into folklore, mythology, theology, psychology, and so on, insofar as these are meant to bear on literature... right down to the first term papers of the class of '75... or, bringing the course of things to this pupil present, right down to this essay. In the very last instant of the film we get a glimpse of giant enumerating machines delivering themselves of quasi-profound remarks about Milton and Shelley...

Again, I am not criticizing this rush of activity, only trying to review it so rapidly and superficially that we can perceive it as a velocity, that is, as movement in a direction. And I make no question that by this process knowledge was mightily improved as well as increased, and intellectual life thereby made the more interesting; no doubt even opinion has thereby been educated and refined. Nonetheless, our survey reveals a rather peculiar situation.

The activity of the great poets, those whose authority and charm survive the fashions of centuries, their language that comes up out of silence and speaks the silence, has produced the flood of our multifarious activities as teachers, scholars, critics, and so on. But there is nothing in this process, once it is set going, that could possibly stop it; nothing from within the process itself. Every explanation is succeeded—this is a law—by an explanation of why the first explanation went fatally wrong; and it is a fact of literary history, said Rosemond Tuve, 'that no one who leaps to his feet to announce a critical error ever sits down without adding some new one.'

And I add something else in the nature of a law. The life of knowledge and criticism becomes as by its own form of entropy always more difficult, never easier. I suspect this is not only, though it is partly, because the life of knowledge and criticism proceeds as much by accumulation as by the substitution of truth for error. It is also the case that knowledge and criticism proceed always in the direction of greater difficulty *because there is no other direction left to them,* because always the easier is assimilated, digested . . . possibly even excreted. Dr. Johnson could satisfy himself about *Hamlet,* though not be altogether satisfied with *Hamlet,* in a page and a half. We cannot do that. Of course, we say, we know more about *Hamlet* than Dr. Johnson did. And that is quite true. But, with a kind of reflexive sadness, what we know is always our own knowledge, never *Hamlet.*

In conclusion, I stress once again that I am trying to picture our situation, not to criticize it. For the first move of the understanding ought to be the silent contemplation of what is, and of how it got to be the way it is. No doubt the teacher of English will always be 'a man who must talk for an hour.' But if his talk is really to do its work, if his pupils are truly to become possessed of some sense of what poetry is and why it is, his speech itself will have to contain much silence. For every use of language about language will tend to produce more language; but the deeper purpose of language is to produce the silence of understanding, the consent between speech and its object, between speaker and hearer, the 'it is as it is' that is the end of every great work.

THE MIRACULOUS
TRANSFORMATIONS OF
MAURITS CORNELIS ESCHER

There is an interface common to science, art, and poetry, but it remains hidden most of the time even from adepts in these skills, in part because they are adepts. Once in a while the truly dialectic artist reveals this border region, this march which may derive its sinister character from the fact that what it defines is simultaneously a part of and apart from the surrounding territories; here many die. Lu Chi says it in his *Wen Fu, or Prose Poem on The Art of Letters*:

> *the men whose eyes exaggerated ran to excess, the men*
> *who would satisfy their minds prized exactitude:*
> *those with a poor command of words had no way through,*
> *those who were versed in dialectic alone had a free course.*

> (Translation and comparative study by E. R. Hughes, Bollingen Series XXIX [New York: Pantheon Books, 1951], pp. 99–100)

The Dutch artist M. C. Escher is one of those versed in dialectic, and his work charmed me from my first experience of it—though that word 'charmed,' if it is to stand, must be allowed its older and magical senses: bemused, enthralled, hypnotized, or bewitched.

Man may or may not be born 'versed in dialectic,' but if he is he loses this trait early enough, presumably in his struggles with language and technique; it is moving to see how Escher began and long remained a sufficiently conventional artist, of great technical dexterity but showing no sign of his specific gift, unless in a preoccupation with great heights and great depths in his early landscapes.

That gift seems to have come on him more or less suddenly, though there are visible tentative beginnings to decisive continuations, in his mid-thirties. I am tempted to connect the revelation of it with his returning home at about that time (1936) from travels in Italy and France, to Baarn, Holland, where he has since remained. He himself writes of his early preoccupation with the technical alone and for its own sake, and of coming to see this state of mind as a delusion: 'then came the moment when it seemed as if I really saw clearly for the first time.' 'Ideas took hold of me which had nothing to do with graphic art, ideas so fascinating that I felt driven to communicate them to others. This could not be done with words, for they were not literary thoughts, but typical mental images which only become understandable to others on being translated into visual images.' At the end of his very lucid Introduction to *The Graphic Work of M. C. Escher* (New York: Duell Sloan & Pearce, 1961), Escher adds this somewhat muted reflection: 'no matter how objective, how impersonal, most of my subjects appear to me, as far as I have been able to discover, few or none of my fellow men seem to be struck in the same way as I am by the things around them.' In the light of this it seems appropriate that his 1954 Exhibition at Amsterdam occurred under the auspices of the International Congress of Mathematicians, one of whom wrote: 'Probably mathematicians will not only be interested in the geometrical motifs; the same playfulness which constantly appears in mathematics in general, and which to a great many mathematicians is the peculiar charm of their subject, will be a more important element.' (M. C. Escher [Amsterdam: Stedelijk Museum, 1954], Cat. No. 118). Even I, having no aptitude for mathematics or training in it, could readily acknowledge this peculiar charm, and have from Escher, in addition to so much else, at least the illusion of understanding what mathematicians pursue with so much pleasure.

I have no aptitude or training in art criticism, either, so I shall preface my reflections only with the information that Escher's work is strictly in the area of graphics: woodcut, wood-engraving, mezzotint, lithograph, and linoleum cut.

In his *Doctor Faustus,* Thomas Mann characterized the music of his hero Adrian Leverkuhn as 'calculation raised to mystery,' and this is a good beginning motto for what Escher has done with the visible world. Carrying to strictly logical extremes what geometry tells us about the relations of solids in space, he produces mystery, absurdity, and sometimes terror. What he tells us, what he compels us to confront, is a situation with two impossible alternative expressions: a) his world cannot be the real world, because the real world doesn't look like that—and yet we see it!—and b) the way in which we are accustomed to seeing the real world is either not true or not exclusively true. His world is the product of artistic illusion, of course. And yet this illusion is supported by the immense authority of mathematic truth, by the forms of the mind itself, and by an absolute submission of the artistic will to inferences from these forms—it is the illusion that geometrizes! The material and formal preoccupations of this world are bounded at one extreme by the five regular polyhedrons, the stereometric forms, to which Escher adds the sphere, considered as made up of an infinite number of flat planes; at the other extreme by thereomorphic patterns—bugs, fish, birds, reptiles, and men—susceptible of rapid or gradual transformation one into another. For example, the interstices of a flight of white birds are filled with a flight of identical black birds flying the other way. Or, in another work, white fish and black birds fill up the spaces alternately along the central horizon; reading up, the fish fade into a white sky, but reading down the birds blend into a black ocean. This preoccupation with metamorphosis is illustrated by a twelve-foot panel read from left to right, beginning with a crossword arrangement of the word itself (Metamorphose) depending on the O, which may be read either down or across, and on the E, which becomes an M when stood on its side. The word pattern transforms into squares, these dissolve into black and white lizards which, losing their shapes in turn, become hexagons on which, presently, realistic bees alight. These bees in successive transformations come to resemble hummingbirds, then other birds, through the flights of which swim a pattern of contrasting fishes going the other way. The alternation of birds and fishes fades into the light and shaded faces of cubes which, when they become regular enough, turn into a town on a hillside; going down the hill the town's cubist character becomes more detailed, more medieval, more antique, until a castle across the moat of a rippled water turns into a castle in chess just as the water becomes an arrangement of cubes with realistically drawn chess pieces—finally, the cubes turn back into contrasting squares which soon transform themselves into the word with which this world began, metamorphose. Having arrived, we may equally well read the picture backward, from right to left.

In beginning this essay I employed such expressions as interface, march, border region, and these terms are appropriate not only to the intellectual world in which this art takes place but to its first principle of design, or of creation, which might be expressed thus: the edge of anything is also the edge of something else, generally antithetical to the first. This leads to a tightly packed creation, a creation according to the twin principles of plenitude and *natura non facit saltum.* In one of these pictures, *Mosaic II,* these principles of composition are so strictly adhered to that only by filling up the spaces between forms with other forms the artist has invented his own monsters! As Escher says of this attempt, which he views as both a task and a game: 'To the draughtsman it seems as if he were not himself the master of the game, but rather as if his creatures assume the freedom to determine their own shape and character.' Seen in the light of that sentence, this picture and others like it offer the visible equivalent of a theory of evolution, in which by marvelously delicate mutual adjustments of form and function the creatures that fill all possibility define each other's nature with their own.

There is another relation that Escher sometimes dramatizes by similar means, and that is the relation between art and life, between the two-dimensional paper and the three-dimensional world; the pictures in which he does this excellently reveal the delicate balance of his allegiance, artistically, to design and to realism at once; there is something both humorous and very sinister about the lizard who emerges from an abstract pattern of lizards on the page of a sketchbook by first putting his scaly claw over the edge of the book and, gradually becoming 'real,' crawls over some objects on the table and back into the sketchbook, where he resumes his abstraction. It is worth noticing, as the artist does about another example, that this is all 'pure fiction,' for 'the paper remains flat.' So, such pictures subtly point out, both 'reality' and 'illusion' take place in the same world, for whose nature perhaps some third term will have to be found. So, in the now celebrated *Drawing Hands* (1948), a piece which may have said something to Steinberg, two realistic hands with pencils are finishing one another's shirt cuffs on a flat page tacked to the table with realistic thumbtacks.

In three beautiful examples—and I wish there might be more—the artist gives hints of a situation in nature possessing these illusionist properties: the situation of water, which you simultaneously see and see through and see reflections from. These, of mud puddle and still pool and rippled pool, are executed with a marvelous delicacy and purity deliberately alluding to Japanese and Chinese methods. If this were all, as the prayer says, it would have been enough. But there is a further

Three Worlds, 1955.
(Courtesy of Escher Foundation — Haags Gemeentemuseum — The Hague.)

adventure that Escher takes us on, into even more problematic and frightening questions of the spirit's complex discovery-and-invention of its world. These examples, which might be thought to begin where Renaissance studies in perspective leave off, have a resemblance to the Ames experiments and other, similar investigations into the premises of perception. For example, in *Another World,* we look into a cube with arched bays in its five visible sides. On three of the flat lintels of these bays, which are drawn with architectural scrupulousness, are perched birds with human heads, and we are shaken to observe that though we are always looking in the same direction, we see one of these birds in elevation, from the side, one from above, and one from below; and the same is true of three curved horns hung from alternate bays. Reading further, through two bays we look across a moonlike landscape to the horizon with planets and stars and comets; through two others we look down on the craters of this landscape; and through the remaining two we see only the sky with its planets, stars, a spiral nebula, and so on. Architecturally, the plane perpendicular to our line of sight has to be read as wall, floor, ceiling, depending on its context.

Ascending and Descending represents a castle viewed in three-quarter perspective from above. A square promenade around its roof is made of an endless stair on which two lines of hooded figures walk endlessly up or down. And yet the roof remains flat; they walk both up *and* down. Escher in his commentary suggests they may be monks, and that this walk is their ritual duty. Of two outcasts who do not join in this 'spiritual exercise' but mope by themselves on balcony and stair he notes: 'They think they know better than their comrades, but sooner or later they will admit the error of their nonconformity.'

There is a more or less striking resemblance to Kafka, here and in other of Escher's works that employ the closed and endless figure to show human purpose as always 'equal and opposite,' where up and down, back and forth are as much the same as not, and 'both directions, though not without meaning, are equally useless.' But there may also be an allusion to Dante's contrasted likeness of the Avaricious and Prodigal (*Inferno* VII) endlessly rolling their meaningless weights against each other around the fourth circle, divided by '*colpa contraria.*' In the decisive example of this series, *Relativity,* the walls of a brick interior are flanked by stairs. But though this world contains the usual threee dimensions at right angles to one another, the conventional priority whereby we view one of these as the floor, and stand on it, is taken away. One of the results most immediately and horrifyingly visible is

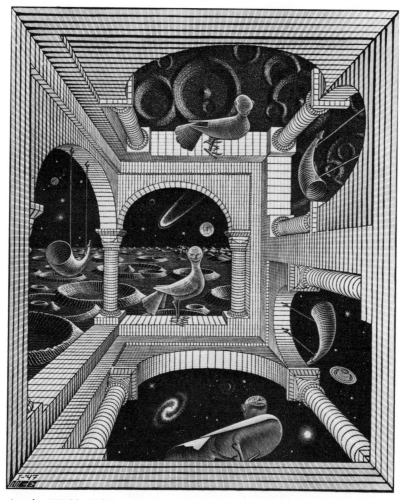

Another World, 1947.
(Courtesy of Escher Foundation—Haags Gemeentemuseum—The Hague.)

the sight of two people going one up and one down the same stairway, which is perfectly natural until you realize that both of them are going in the same direction. I imagine it as the signature of a perfectly dialectical intelligence to see no reason why risers should not be treads or treads be risers.

The same device occurs in *House of Stairs,* where two marches that mirror one another are made by a quite new species of monster, the curl-up or wheel bug (Pedalternorotandomovens centroculatus articulosus), which came by spontaneous generation from the artist's mind 'out of dissatisfaction with the absence, from nature, of any creature using the wheel-form as a means of locomotion.'

Let one last example serve for the emblem of all. Three spheres, horizontally disposed with reference to one another. The one on our right is opaque, milky, suggestive of an egg even though not (from this angle) egg-shaped. The one on our left is either transparent or reflecting, but vaguely. The one in the center is a globular mirror, in the midst of which is Escher seated at a desk drawing his self-portrait. His extremely high forehead is owing to the curve of the glass, but otherwise he looks no less an ordinary human being than you, reader, and I.

Upon this extraordinary image I had thought to poetize endlessly, or as near as no matter. But now I come to it I decide that silence is better, for this picture represents to me one of those first and last secrets which everyone has to discover the meaning of for himself and as he best may. I am led to think once more of Dante, who refuses to interpret a somewhat similar self-portrait, wherein Virgil protects him from the Gorgon by closing his eyes:

> O voi, che avete gl'intelletti sani,
> mirate la dottrina, che s'asconde
> sotto il velame degli versi strani!

Whether things are or are not as they seem is an enduring preoccupation of art. Sometimes, to say that things are not what they appear to be is a consolation, for it suggests that wisdom is hidden, and that in its turn suggests that only the wise can find it, and that in its own turn suggests that we ourselves are wise for having said that things are not what they seem. At other times, our consolation may come from saying that things are exactly what they seem, there is no deceit in the world. Temperamentally, we may be inclined to the

Reptiles, 1943.

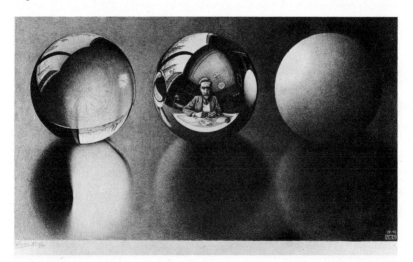

Three Spheres, 1946.
(Courtesy of Escher Foundation – Haags Gemeentemuseum – The Hague.)

surfaces, or we may be inclined to the depths, but both temperaments have to ask about how the surfaces and the depths are related, if indeed they have anything to do with one another at all.

Shakespeare, in his riddling way, supplies a paradigm or model for this question, which he worked out in various situations of human agony: is the truth of this life found in love or in cynical intelligence? in an absolute idealism extending to disbelief in the evidence of the senses (as when Troilus is compelled to see, and refuses to believe, that Cressida is betraying him), or in an equally absolute materialism and practicality extending to disavowal of any ideal beyond the self and its desires (as in Edmund's speech about the stars)?

Othello is perhaps the simplest of the decisive examples. Othello is deceived by Iago's arguments and demonstrations exactly because wisdom in this world says things are not what they seem. Desdemona seems innocent, and this very seeming becomes the strongest proof of a monstrous guilt. But Desdemona turns out—too late—to have been exactly what she seemed, innocent. And there was a wisdom beyond the wisdom of this world that Othello betrayed in betraying her.

In the same way, in Proust, the relations of appearance and truth often have three stages. In the first, we believe what we see or are told. In the second, we *see through* that false appearance, of beauty, of idealism, of dishonesty, of hypocrisy, to the truth opposed, the truth beneath the surface. And we continue in our new wisdom, perhaps for twenty years, before one day discovering that the perception of the first stage was accurate, though perhaps not complete, and that it was our wisdom itself, our psychological penetration, our great diagnostic acumen, that was a folly and a delusion.

These great masters of the secrets of the heart, the mind, the world, may at first sight look rather far from the preoccupations of Maurits Cornelis Escher. But I think that's not so. Perhaps a certain appearance of inhumanity, even of cruelty and mockery, in his marvelously ingenious works is there to evoke a certain humanity in our response. He, too, is playing always, like Shakespeare, like Proust, with the simple but endless problem of true illusions, a problem affecting equally technique and the spirit. With those others, he seems to say to us, Look! don't be so smug. Try to go at least one illusion beyond the illusion you have inherited or accepted by custom, by habit, by laziness; you will see that all things change their signs; it may be not a simple business of illusion and reality; it may be a more subtle business than that, and worthier of its playful creator. A moiré, for example, where two slightly discrepant grids produce when put together a third thing unlike either. Or else something so simple as the moebius strip, which he is preoccupied with in a number of his works, that in an instant demolishes our perfect certainty that we know the inside of a matter from its outside.

This lesson, which is also the lesson above all of Alfred North Whitehead in philosophy, bears the human instruction, the very humane instruction, not to despair, not to give up, but to continue the search with as much humor and patience as possible. Doing so, oddly enough, we shall be as much with the evidence as against it, and one day one simple step more will reveal the world as absolutely other, its own and living Other World.

—1963

Acknowledgment

I am grateful to Mr. Alan Fern for the loan of the Amsterdam catalogue, to Mr. Fern and Mrs. Jeanne Tifft for showing me the Escher prints in the Library of Congress, and to Mr. Sidney Mickelson of the Mickelson Gallery, Washington, D. C., for allowing me to look over at leisure the gallery's large collection.

THE WINTER ADDRESSES
OF KENNETH BURKE
with some Thoughts about
Interpretation

჻⸙ᲢᲯᏩᎾ჻

First off, it will be convenient to have the text before us:

> *College Garden Apartments*
> *5831 Walnut Street,*
> 3 *Apt. 24*
> *Pittsburgh, PA 15232*
>
> *University of Pittsburgh*
> 6 *Department of English*
> *526 Cathedral of Learning*
> *Oakland*
> 9 *Pittsburgh, PA 15260*

One imagines that even a superficial reader will respond immediately to the appeal of this muted little lyric, so full as it is of verbal play, subtle variation, and incremental repetition. But to the reader steeped in the Judaeo-Christian tradition, the reader whose delight is response, interpretation, the unfolding of what is infolded, there is much more here to meet the mind than at first meets the eye: Compacted into nine short lines we find the speaker's cryptic parable of his religious history and of that of a larger part of mankind, of which he is the type.

The method is threefold: Paratactic, elliptical, and allusive. Paratactic, in that the items, as of a catalogue, are given without syntactical or causal relation—*post hoc,* with the reader left to infer the *propter hoc.* Elliptical, in that what is omitted may be of as great import as what is said. And allusive, of course, chiefly to the scriptures and their sacred history.

Our interpretative method, correspondingly, will demand much tact. For as there is no overt, coherent narrative, we shall have to proceed by comparing and contrasting elements that appear in both stanzas and testing these for their precise degree of likeness and difference, or likeness-in-difference. For convenience we prefer to go from the more obvious to the more recondite; hence we shall leave number symbolism until the end. And, one last preliminary point: the two stanzas may be related indifferently as either a drama developing in time or as an arrangement in space; we shall try to show how both readings harmonize.

We begin in a *garden* with two trees in it. The *walnut,* bearing edible fruit, is mentioned at once; the *oak,* not bearing edible fruit, is withheld till line eight, almost the end of the poem, and partly concealed as *Oakland.* The reference to Genesis 3 is of course obvious, and we anticipate being told a version of the Fall of Man, though with certain highly individual features; Eve, for instance, does not appear, nor does the Serpent; anticipating further, we hazard a guess at the significance of these omissions, that this story of the Fall is being told with a peculiarly exclusive emphasis on knowledge, or *learning* (line seven), hence perhaps—but this is inference—with an exclusively masculine and even onanistic emphasis on a certain pride, balanced by a certain sterility, in the human project of mastering the world by knowing.

So. We begin in the Garden, alone. Considering a little more closely the first line, 'College Garden Apartments,' we compare the innocence of 'college' in the first stanza with the somewhat lofty, not to say pretentious, claim implicit in 'university' in the second, noting as a couple of corresponsive changes that we also go from *garden* to *cathedral,* from *walnut* to *oak,* and from *apartment* with its idea of being set *apart* whether for good or ill to *department* with its ominous hint of *departure,* or being sent forth. It goes with this that the idea behind *college,* if this be not to consider too curiously, comes from L. *legare,* to be chosen or sent as deputy. This will give a clue to one more significant omission as we note that we have been taken from *garden* to *cathedral* with no mention whatever of the incarnation, crucifixion, and resurrection of Christ as the savior of mankind; the inference, of course, is that the speaker views himself as a secular son of God exiled from the garden with the purpose of redeeming mankind by knowledge alone, by building not Jerusalem but the *Cathedral of Learning,* which evidently, is the eulogistic name for what the Bible names dyslogistically the Tower of Babel. (There may nevertheless be a kind of grotesque or parodied kind of crucifixion concealed in *English,* if, joycing the word as other writers have done before this, we hear 'the anguish languish'; but we shall not insist on this.)

The story told in time is complemented by the relation set forth in space, where the two stanzas, or *addresses,* relate as *home* and *office,* or *work* ('in the sweat of thy face shalt thou eat bread'—Genesis 3:19), so that as temporally we proceed from innocence to experience, spatially we endure a tension between innocence and experience, though it is well to note that both, according to the refrain of lines four and nine, come equivocally under the power of the Devil and the Father, as is clearly made to appear in *Pittsburgh,* or City of the Pit, and PA, or the fatherland (whose Jupiterian emblem is also the *oak* of *Oakland*). A plaintive communication from the poet will confirm this reading, as well as serving to introduce the difficult subject of number symbolism: 'The difference betwixt thirty-two and sixty makes me wonder whether I may be housed farther from headquarters'—sc. heaven,— 'than I had hoped.'

The poet's propensity to lisp in numbers is not, for me, the happiest aspect of his production. For example, does 'Apt. 24' refer to his eager setting-forth on the road to knowledge at that age, to his aptitude? I do not know. But I can see some reason for the submergence of part of the underthoughts in cipher, for that part is about relations of orthodoxy and heresy.

Very briefly, then, 5831 breaks into five plus eight equal thirteen, and the reversed thirteen, or three in one, of the Trinity. Bad luck and the sacred. 15232 also adds up to thirteen, as does 526 in line seven; while the last number, concluding the whole, totals fourteen, with a hint of the one in four, the quaternity, opposed to the Trinity in some Gnostic and Manichaean beliefs, or religions with an exclusive emphasis on *knowledge.* What to make of that last despairing zero, I confess, I do not know, but the rest of the last line seems to me to acknowledge the reality of evil in the City of the Pit, while stoically or minimally affirming the presiding presence of PA the Father.

That joke, which perhaps went on a touch too long as it is, might have been even longer had it not been interrupted by the visit of a student from Porlock in distress about a term paper. I am not at all sure just now what lessons if any may be drawn from it concerning poems and interpretations, but on the principle that he goes farthest who knows not where he is going, I am ready to launch out more or less at random.

First, then, with some observations about how the foregoing happened to happen.

Kenneth Burke and I have exchanged, I guess, about a letter a week for a good many years now, and in the course of these letters it sometimes happens that one will include a new verse, on which the other is expected to comment and sometimes does. So when I opened a letter from Kenneth and saw that the reverse of the page bore a couple of groups of indented lines, I suppose I was already anticipating a poem while I read the beginning of the letter, following the hard-nosed definition laid down by Jeremy Bentham, that when the lines run all the way to the right margin it is prose; when this fails to happen, it is poetry. So that when I turned the page and saw that the indented lines were really giving me my friend's addresses in Pittsburgh where he was to spend the winter months, it seems that my rhapsode's interpreting mood was still strong enough to override the plain fact of the matter. Obviously, though, it could not have done anything of the sort without some help from the matter itself.

Then a strange thing happened. I knew instantly that I could, and would, interpret these addresses as though they constituted a poem. Not only that, but I knew instantly the main lines of the interpretation, and that I would certainly write them out on the morrow; and so in fact it went. Confirming something I had frequently observed about interpretation, whether in the classroom or when writing: that interpretation is rapid, rhapsodic, sudden, unexpected, having all the signs of being inspired—a distant, impersonal, yet excited seeing, or *realizing,* such as goes with the composition of a poem you *know* is going to work, is going to come clear. (It need not affect the argument that this feeling of inspiration and immediacy of knowledge, whether in composing or interpreting, may turn out to have been mistaken; it nevertheless exists and is a happiness while it lasts.)

So that is more or less how it happened. Now I wonder if it is possible to say at all what happened, or anything about this kind of happening in general.

The objections I want from the reader just now, the ones I feel confident of being able to deal with, are two:

1. But it isn't a poem.
2. You are reading things into it.

As to the first, I should reply that one is not so certain these days as formerly what is a poem and what isn't a poem. And I point out that your confident assertion as to what it *isn't,* a poem, is predicated upon your knowing what it really *is,* a couple of addresses. If you didn't know that, you would certainly sound less assured, and might find no identifiable ground at all for saying it is not a poem. Maybe its so looking exactly not like a poem is exactly what confers its poetic character and title? No, this isn't spinning paradoxes, or not altogether. The poet's task has generally been conceded to be hard, but it may be so described as to make it logically impossible: Make an object recognizable as an individual of the class p for poem, but make it in such a way that it resembles no other individual of that class. It's not really that bad, for in fact poems come in waves of kind, not to mention in imitation of other poems; but with a sufficient emphasis on individuality it might be that bad.

Now as to the second objection: All right, it's a poem, if you like but you're reading things into it. Well, I should be very happy to have someone bring up that old crux, for it's where I want to be, where I want us to start.

In literary criticism the charge that you're reading things into the poem—things, it is understood, that aren't there—and defining the word 'there' in that context might give some bother—is so automatically accepted as the sin against the holy ghost that I have never heard anyone say what needs to be said: Why yes, of course I am, what else would you do with a poem? (On this, a student with whom I had been reading, not a whole book, but two or three sentences with conversation about these, gave me this surprised definition: 'I see what reading is; it's putting together what it says with what you've got.' And surely this is the right place for a motto by Wallace Stevens: 'The poem must resist the intelligence / Almost successfully.')

I shall go further now, and assert that the two addresses have become a poem, though they weren't one before, largely in virtue of my having read things into them; things that are now there even if they weren't there before. And I shall go much too far, as well, and assert that you can no longer read those two addresses together purely as addresses, without taking into account the sort of syntax of elements I have made explicit, such as for instance that between garden and cathedral. It's a joke, if you like, but it's a pretty dirty joke. This is so for a reason that is rarely if ever said aloud, maybe because when said aloud it becomes self-evident: that interpretation, of its nature, is or at least overlaps with misinterpretation; were that not so, it would be either fact or revelation. To go with that, here is a definition to deal with: a poem is a dream containing its own interpretation. Which means you have to tease the interpretation out of the dream, but in awareness that while doing so you are dreaming too. Concerning this, Claude Lévi-Strauss said something thoughtful to this effect: it matters little, he said, whether I am interpreting certain myths, or whether in truth they are interpreting my mind to me; what matters, he added, is to get a view of 'the mind imitating itself as object' (paraphrased from *The Raw and the Cooked* [New York: Harper & Row, 1969]). On this point I too have thought that in general I do not much care for myths, which before they have been treated by a great poet are so often dull, confused, rambling, repetitive—but I do care ever so much for the myths we are sometimes able to make up about what they mean. For it is there that you get a glimpse of a theme that must surely be of the greatest interest to teachers: how meaning gets into the world at all.

It is time for an illustration of how this works, if it does work, to set against my two addresses, and by good luck I've remembered one short enough to fit in here, and clear enough, if not to convince, at any rate to make the position clear in turn.

THE JEWEL STAIRS GRIEVANCE

The jewelled steps are already quite white with dew,
It is so late that the dew soaks my gauze stockings,
And I let down the crystal curtain
And watch the moon through the clear autumn.

To any untaught reader, I daresay, this is transparently a visual (and tactile) poem of the generically 'oriental' kind that has been fashionable quite often in recent times; it is an 'imagist' poem, we might say, even down to its 'jeweled' quality, a clear little moment demanding no interpretation but only, perhaps, a connoisseurish appreciation of its delicacy: interpretation would be not only far-fetched and uncertain, we think, but vulgar as well.

The poem is in fact a translation, or imitation, by Ezra Pound from Rihaku (which I've been told is the Japanese name for Li Po), and Pound adds the following Note:

> Jewel stairs, therefore a palace. Grievance, therefore there is something to complain of. Gauze stockings, therefore a court

lady, not a servant, who complains. Clear autumn, therefore he has no excuse on account of weather. Also she has come early, for the dew has not merely whitened the stairs, but has soaked her stockings. The poem is especially prized because she utters no direct reproach.

(Ezra Pound, *Selected Poems*,
edited by T S. Eliot [London:
Faber & Faber, 1928], p. 111)

This is the sort of thing that separates sheep from goat and Nominalist from Realist, though even when you have the two parties sorted out it remains hard enough to tell t'other from which. But, putting it as crudely as possible: Does the meaning, the reiterated inference 'therefore' from the facts, improve the poem? Or were you happier with just the text of the poem alone? Or—the tricky third thing—could you remain happy with just the words of the poem after someone had told you it had a hidden meaning but refused to tell you what it was? Pound's answer seems to me decisive at least for the tradition out of which the poem emerged: it is 'especially prized because she utters no direct reproach.'

And some generalized corollary of that answer is also the answer honorably given by teachers of literature on our professional occasions. Mr. MacLeish's celebrated slogan to the contrary, a poem must be and mean at once. Doing that is a tricky thing, too, and I propose to give the last part and instance of this essay to the mystery of it.

Although the 'intentional fallacy' is also numbered among our deadly sins, we do all the same believe that poems are intentional, and that the intentions of them do belong 'somehow' to their makers, even if we are prepared to concede that the makers were not thinking about intention, or meaning, during the course of composition. One part of the mystery of poetry is that it does not clearly distinguish the plan from its fulfillment. There is in general no blueprint to be followed in other materials; the blueprint, in poetry, is the building. That is because, say, the poet makes an image, in which meanings somehow inhere, and which it is the honorable work of interpretation to distinguish in the poem, without dividing them from the poem.

Two brief instances. Shakespeare's 107th Sonnet, 'Not mine owne feares nor the prophetick soule...' is a mysterious poem which has evoked and provoked comment about its meaning in just the degree, perhaps, that it has resisted the same. The poem must resist the intelligence almost successfully. Its fifth line, 'The mortall Moone hath her eclipse indur'de,' has received more attention than most, possibly because it is more uncertain than most. Some propose it as a means of dating the Sonnets by literal lunar eclipses visible from the Greenwich Meridian (unhappily, there were a good many of those), and at least one writer, Leslie Hotson, has argued for a date on the ground that 'the mortall Moone' represents the Armada, which was at least believed to have approached the English shore in a crescent formation. While others, arguing that the Moone is conventional poetic talk for Elizabeth, propose to date the Sonnets that way. Unhappily, the line contains an equivocation fatal to the argument, for it could mean either 'Elizabeth has recovered from a serious head cold which might well have been fatal' or that she had died. Needless to say, all these interpretations are such as divide the meaning from the poem, rather than distinguishing the meaning in the poem.

The following exchange between Robert Frost and myself took place only in a dream of mine, but may be illustrative all the same. I, the eager interpreter, said of 'Spring Pools' that it was 'obviously' about one's growth from young to old, from potency to act, and the pathos, or even tragedy, attendant upon even the most successful completion of the process. To which, in my dream, the poet smiled and said that he rather thought he was writing about capillary action in trees. Of course, I should contend, at least in waking hours, we were both right, he about fact and I about inference from fact. It is always the poet's privilege to retire upon what the poem says, for that is his business; while the interpreter, so long as he knows the fact of the poem and does not contradict it, has the liberty, and indeed the duty, of ranging widely indeed in the drawing of inferences from the fact. On this account I have devised and tried to obey the following instruction about writing: The saying as clear as you can make it—for that is your duty and your gift—; the meaning as mysterious as may be. For the universe is so.

My first instance was a pair of addresses treated as a poem. The illustration was a pure and perfect one because in the first place it had no author, so could have no intention other than what I supplied and made coherent by interpretation. My last instance seems to me somewhat the same and yet reversed. It has to be a poem of my own, both because about a poem of my own I can assure you that I did not know of any abstract intention, or blueprint, while writing it, and also because for some reason I can remember and tell you, by a kind of biographical archaeology, about the source of practically everything in it; in fact, because it is 'the same and yet reversed,' I will give you the heap of elements first, and the poem only afterward.

In chronological succession as nearly as I can remember, here are the elements.

1938 or so. A friend told me of having seen the terse inscription 'to die is gain' on a young girl's tombstone in a New Haven graveyard. That the phrase is from Philippians 1 is something I didn't know for many years, and doesn't seem to matter anyhow.

At about the same time I was first studying Dante, and reading of the leaves of Sybil's prophecies scattered by wind and right afterward, also in the last canto of the *Paradiso,* the famous vision of the volume of the universe whose leaves appear to us on earth as scattered.

1950 or so. Driving among the mountains of Vermont in Fall, my wife said that the varicolored forests resembled the reverse side of a tapestry. An unconsidered trifle I naturally snapped up and saved for some fifteen years.

From the fifties also. One observed that there began to be Fall Foliage Tours, with people coming to Vermont from as far as New York and Boston, in buses, to take pictures of the brilliant spectrum of the leaves, which, incidentally, they did through tinted windows.

1960 or so. I came to know Robert Frost one summer toward the last of his life, and somewhat against the odds we got to be friends, though we did not meet often. No anecdotes, but it may have been the sympathetic vibration of two misanthropes; and the poem was written in the autumn after his death. As though in slight defiance, its last line, about a pair of maples I had walked under every autumn for many years, was ready and waiting to fulfill its poem; Frost held that it couldn't be done that way. In a well-known discussion called 'The Figure a Poem Makes,' he described that figure as beginning in delight and ending in wisdom, insisted that its outcome be unforeseen but predestined from the first image of the original mood, and added with perhaps a touch of petulance, 'It is but a trick poem and no poem at all if the best of it was thought first and saved for the last.' I incline generally to agree, but may say in extenuation that if that line was thought of first and saved for the last, that included the fact that I had tried it in other poems over several years and always destroyed them for exactly the reason that though it was obviously a last line it was not *their* last line, being so far and away too good for them.

So. There are the elements. Here is the poem.

FOR ROBERT FROST, IN THE AUTUMN, IN VERMONT

All on the mountains, as on tapestries
Reversed, their threads unreadable though clear,
The leaves turn in the volume of the year.
Your land becomes more brilliant as it dies.
The puzzled pilgrims come, car after car,
With cameras loaded for epiphanies;
For views of failure to take home and prize,
The dying tourists ride through realms of fire.

'To die is gain,' a virgin's tombstone said.
That was New England, too, another age
That put a higher price on maidenhead
If brought in dead; now on your turning page
The lines blaze with a constant light, displayed
As in the maples' cold and fiery shade.

About a decade after writing that, I think I've some idea how its elements fit together, and even why. But perhaps after being so very voluble an explicator of both a non-poem and the poetry of other poets, I should properly fall silent about this one, taking to heart the instruction I paraphrased for you earlier:

As with a dream interpreted by one still sleeping,
The interpretation is only the next room of the dream.

QUIDNUNC THE POET
AND MR. GIGADIBS

A bad thing happened to me recently, bringing with it the humiliating conviction of my age and obsolescence: I read *The New York Times Book Review,* and found it too avant-garde.

Not all of it, not for example the lead review where Muriel Spark is praised for having composed the simile 'a mind like a blade,' and for having a character in a story think, 'There is no health, she thought, for me, outside of honesty.' That much originality and that much psychological penetration, even that many commas, I am still able to keep up with.

Nor do I have any trouble understanding my being somewhat *démodé* when it is explained to me in plain language by a reviewer who says: 'The forties and fifties were a bad time, isolated and provincial . . . a time of teaching English literature for very little money at some hideous little college in the woods.' Yep, that's me, I say as the reviewer continues, 'The new scene is urban and "anti-academic."' That too I can accept, though I wonder about the quotation marks; does he believe the new scene is really urban but only sort of pretending to be anti-academic? A note about this reviewer says that he has just completed a novel. He writes criticism and teaches at The State University of New York at Stony Brook.

But the real revelation of how far I had fallen behind came from a reading of Mr. Gigadibs's review of Quidnunc's book of poems. It happened that I had been reading this book during the past week, and finding it a comfortably familiar sort of composition, openly acknowledging such influences as Blake, Whitman, Pound. It is very earnest and high-minded and rather religiose in tone; the poet gives a sermon against President Johnson, grieves for the victims of a very wicked war, excoriates Clark Kerr and Chancellor Strong (whom he thinks of as a dragon, possibly because Blake would have viewed him that way), writes a great deal of poetry about the writing of poetry, and so on. I thought I was getting on famously, understanding fine—save for a line

in Greek, which a friend skilled in such matters tells me has an error in
every word—and now comes Mr. Gigadibs with the humbling news
that begins 'Quidnunc must certainly be our most difficult active poet.'
Suppressing a shudder at the thought of all those inactive poets who
must be more difficult still—otherwise why the precaution? or does he
mean passive poets?—I read on, and learn that to read 'with any
immediate grace' what I had foolishly thought I was reading 'would
require Norman O. Brown's knowledge of the arcane mixed with Ezra
Pound's grasp of poetics.' Well, I certainly don't have those. Mr.
Gigadibs goes on:

> Though Quidnunc avows himself a purely derivative poet, his
> capacities are monstrous and have taken a singular direction: . . .
> Quidnunc the range of affection is great and nothing is barred
> entrance from the 'field' of composition.

There are those quotation marks again. Does Mr. Gigadibs believe
in the existence of a field of composition or not? It is surely a notion
familiar enough by now not to need so gingerly a pair of tongs to pick
it up with. Mr. Gigadibs too teaches English at Stony Brook.

'Though Quidnunc avows himself a purely derivative poet . . .' Back
in the bad forties and fifties, poets used to be called derivative by
critics; they never *avowed* it of themselves, and even critics were rarely
so rude as to say a derivative poet was *purely* so; for it was possible that
something of his own had got in maybe by accident. But that red
herring must not be allowed to divert us from the true post-modernism
of the sentence, which is in its construction: instead of the antithesis we
might expect—'he says he's derivative, but I say he's not'—Mr.
Gigadibs springs the planned surprise of an irrelevance:

> Though Quidnunc avows himself a purely derivative poet, his
> capacities are monstrous and have taken a singular direction: . . .

Can this mean that when capacities are monstrous enough to move in
a direction at all they might be expected—if one didn't watch out—to
move in more than one direction at once? Singular indeed. As to the
last clause, the one after the colon which characterizes the direction:

> . . . in Quidnunc the range of affection is great and nothing is
> barred entrance from the 'field' of composition.

—does this, can it, mean that he likes a good many different things and doesn't refuse to put them in his poems? Mr. Gigadibs's next two sentences do not altogether remove the difficulties already raised:

> The structure of (these poems) is the 'grand collage.' It is for this
> reason that his poetry has been called cluttered and self-defeating,
> even swollen and diversive by his admirers.

Divisive? diversified? (or even, considering the poems, de-versified?) It is curious that a dictionary so careful as to give things like 'diversipedate' and 'diversisporous' should fail of 'diversive.' What could the admirers have meant? that the poetry was diverting? And isn't there a comma missing, as though the strain of inventing 'diversive' had been so great that something had to give immediately after it? Even the placement of 'even' is odd; for surely the force of the thought is that these nasty things are said about Quidnunc's poetry even by his admirers, making us wonder what stronger terms his detractors could find, if he has any. But in Mr. Gigadibs's prose it is the admirers that thus intensify from one epithet to the next their hostility against the work they are said to be admiring.

Now Mr. Gigadibs himself is one of the admirers, and he begins the next paragraph by telling us that we shall think these nasty thoughts only if we persist in our stupid old habit of reading the poems from beginning to end; that at least is the sense I take from his sentence: 'These qualifications are only relevant [his word order] if we are unable to transcend our purely linear sense of what a poem should be.' If we achieve this transcendence, and read properly—not in a purely linear sense—the poems which make up the largest part of the book, we shall be able to share with Mr. Gigadibs the following revelations:

> Form in (these poems) is a four-dimensional process, constantly
> active, never passive, moving through time with the poet. The
> poems are music-based rather than ideational, the rhythms con-
> centrated in time, avoiding any strict sense of measure. . . .

This is impressive stuff indeed, but I have questions. The dictionary says that 'ideational' means 'consisting in, or referring to, thought of objects not immediately present to the senses'; is Quidnunc then like the philosophers in Swift who carried with them the things they wished to speak about? Or does it mean that he never thinks? Another question: when one writes or reads a poem, does one expect its rhythms, whether concentrated or diffuse, to be elsewhere than in time? Leaving aside whether an object-in-language, either lying flat on the page or spoken aloud, can possibly be four-dimensional, if it moves with the poet where else than in time could it possibly do so? And another: You can avoid strict measure, but how do you avoid a strict sense of measure? In any event, what about the measure of these lines?

> Slowly the toiling images will arise,
> Shake off, as if it were debris,
>   the unnecessary pleasures of our lives
> And all times and intents of peaceful men
> Reduce to an interim, a passing play. . . .

It is true that Quidnunc doesn't often do this, though in the same passage he has extended quotations from Spenser and Shakespeare that do it for him; what Mr. Gigadibs means may be illustrated also from the same passage:

> In the carved panel of the sarcophagus from Golgoi (The Metropolitan Museum of Art, *Handbook of The Cesnoa Collection of Antiquities from Cyprus.* As given in Cook, *Zeus,* vol. two, part one, p. 718).

Finally—or not finally at all, but as far as I am going with him just now—Mr. Gigadibs, somewhat in the voice of Eliot introducing schoolchildren to the *Cantos* of Pound, sees clearly and says sadly and a little wearily that if we don't understand Quidnunc the trouble is that we just plain don't know enough:

> Another more obvious stumbling point for the reader is Quidnunc's aggressive syncretism: he is personal rather than confessional and writes within a continuity of tradition. It simply helps to be familiar with Dante, Blake, mythography, medieval history, H. D., William Carlos Williams, Pound, Stein, Zukofsky, Olson, Creeley, and Levertov.

No doubt a continuity of tradition containing ten or twelve items and beginning with Dante and Blake will have to trail off a little toward the end; but a continuity of tradition having one representative around 1300, another around 1800, and all the rest in the last ten minutes may appear as somewhat failing of tradition and continuousness together. As for the difference between being personal and being confessional, I'm no more certain of it than of other of Mr. Gigadibs's 112° antitheses, but after long thought I was able to produce a possible illustration:

I have bad breath. I am being confessional.
You have bad breath. I am being personal.

THOUGHTS ON FIRST PASSING
THE HUNDREDTH PAGE OF
FINNEGANS WAKE

꙳ ꙳ ꙳

'You is feeling like you was lost in the bush, boy?'

As far as I have got in this book, I've had every feeling in the book: fascination and despair, pleasure, charm, bitter resentment, resistance to reading one inch farther; great admiration, terrible boredom, simple fury at frustration, childish delight at resolving this or that small trouble, and so on. I haven't that ideal insomnia (p. 120), and I'd swear there are stretches of half a dozen pages where Joyce keeps the sentence from concluding by every device known to man only *pour me faire enrager* (the first question in the quiz, pp. 126–39, to which the answer is 'Finn MacCool,' is a resounding instance and a bloody bore as well); yet when I see that this is what he's doing I generally have to grin and go on—the grin largely affectionate if keeping the ghost of a snarl.

Chiefly, though, I am amazed. The energy and geniality of the book are just amazing; there's nothing like it in literature, and comparisons (Rabelais, Burton, Shikespower, Seudodanto, Anonymoses) don't seem to mean much. It's a help, too, that so many places are so helplessly funny: the guided tour of the Willingdone Museyroom, the dialogue of Mutt and Jute, the interview with Sylvia Silence the girl detective; and not only such set pieces, but ever so many passing moments else.

Against that, I keep the sense I began with—that once you've got the idea, the stuff is a good deal easier to write than to read, and maybe even more fun as well. Of course, Joyce had the idea. But it's odd, all the same, that this way of using language never took any real hold among writers; it would seem a natural for people who keep complaining that the center will not hold . . . poets ought to have taken to it right off. I guess the difficulty might be the same that people experienced when they tried to imitate some of the methods of composition in *Ulysses,* especially the celebrated and misnamed 'stream of consciousness': they found not only that what streams do is run down, but also that their very own characters were merely thinking the thoughts of Leopold Bloom and Stephen Dedalus. So here. If you disorganized your language in this way you would almost helplessly do so in the same dactylic and anapestic rhythms. Besides, a major point of the book is that there's only one dream; Joyce has dreamed it for us, and we shall have to wait till the end of days for the second coming and the redreamer (oops).

I remember getting a great deal of pleasure from hearing passages read aloud by a drunken painter (his audience wasn't so sober either). Taken in a relaxed and boozy way, the book is marvelous at producing the illusion of understanding; traveling at that speed you don't unpack the portmanteaux, you just listen to the clicking of the wheels. For study, however, I've found it handy indeed to have commentaries and specialized dictionaries and the like, although I also have some doubts about their ultimate usefulness, which I'll come to later. Meanwhile, I gratefully acknowledge the help of the authors of *A Skeleton Key* and of Miss Glasheen in her *Second Census of Finnegans Wake.* Also of numerous writers who give me a sense of the whole without dealing so closely with the text, beginning with John Peale Bishop (who must have written his splendid review-essay about the day the book came out) and coming up to Burgess's *Re Joyce.*

That the book should be so full of shit doesn't seem to be much of a bother, possibly because the leading thematic image of history as a dungheap, garbage midden, tumulus, barrow, and so on is so pleasantly what Kenneth Burke would call a comic corrective to those newspapery notions that confuse the sordid with tragedy. This image has its marvelous figurative extensions, too, as in the account of Waterloo, where the sounds of battle are also the sounds of defecation (cf. chamberpot-thundermug; and our author, in a first fine instance of his flair for such expansions and reductions, called his early poems *Chambermusic*).

In a number of ways that puzzle and a little bother me, there is a curious doubleness to the book. Not in the details, where there is often a greater multiplicity than that without causing trouble, but in the idea of the whole. I'll try to explain.

You can either read along, preferably aloud, getting a sort of sense of what's going forward (not always, but often); or you can focus on the resolution of little bits, single words or single phrases; but if you do that you very often forget what the whole situation is and lose the narrative.

Again, you can either read with the help of commentaries which emphasize the large cyclic and repetitive motions of the whole, or (with or without commentaries) try to figure it out inch by inch (quite literally; it helps to have a bookmark keyed to the numbers of the lines). For instance, you can either hold recurring details and motifs in your head till you begin to know something about the centers from which the single reference radiates, which is a horrible hard business, or you can stop the first time you see something famous and clearly labeled *thematic* (such as numbers: 1132, 29, the Four) and look it up in a commentary—from which, by the way, you are liable not to get so very much joy as all that.

Similarly, it is ever so easy to acquire a glib familiarity with Viconian cycles, the coincidence of opposites, the reciprocity between death and resurrection; but when you have come to know such things you haven't come to know much more than a set of clichés that in one way and another have been the cant terms of world historians from Augustine to Spengler. And if you don't consent to believe that mastering this sort of junk is learning, you are left with one anecdote after another in which just this sort of junk is (often marvelously) exemplified in street fights, landscapes, archaeological surveys, rumors, lectures in paleography and textual criticism, et cetera (and incidentally, for all Joyce's emphasis on low life he seems most often most at home—so far as I've read, anyhow—doing a parody of the pedant).

The same doubleness appears among readers, in the division of opinion (one could scarcely view it as an argument, for the two sides don't talk to one another) between those who want to read *Finnegans Wake* 'as a novel' and the other party—roughly speaking, the cabalists, the cryptanalysts, the people who use the book more or less as one might use *The Book of Changes*. (Like the man I met once who earnestly assured me that he wasn't at all interested in literature, only in *Finnegans Wake*. Well, some days I feel the same way about music and Bach.) A learned friend, who tells me, and I believe him, that he has read all 'the literature' without ever having more than glanced through the book itself, is firmly of the opinion that it can and must be read 'as a novel' about an aging man, his wife and children, and—what? The resolution, I guess, during a night's dreaming, of his troubles in reconciling himself to the passage into old age and thence out of life. But against this idea of reading it 'for the story,' as it were, you have the equally firm opinion of Thornton Wilder, which tells us severely that we are not really in the book at all until we've logged a thousands hours at it. My trouble just now is that I don't find anywhere, as far as I've gone, a place where the two extreme views harmonize: where, that is, the maximum rub-your-nose-in-it-complexity-unto-chaos of how things really happen in this vale of tears becomes one with the absolute of abstraction also claimed for the work, the place at which history really does repeat itself—and does nothing else—because every story is a family story.

But now, having expressed these doubts about how the book works, I should say on the other side that *Finnegans Wake* is doing one of the things a masterpiece probably ought to do, which is to make me think some thoughts I had not thought before. This is not the same thing as 'original thoughts,' or 'profound thoughts,' or 'thoughts beyond the reaches of our souls'; only things I had not thought before. I shall try to put the few of them down here.

In ever so many ways—by its grammar and even its spelling, by its being read silently and alone, in a contemplative frame of mind—it is the nature of printed literature to confirm us in a number of related beliefs, which may or may not be delusions, concerning the way in which language mediates between a human being and the world. These beliefs, which Joyce, bless him, compels his reader to inspect, might be characterized in different ways by each of us, but I should name them as follows:

(1) That language is a mental phenomenon alone. (2) That literature belongs to and is done exclusively by 'the still and mental parts.' (3) That the shapes assigned to words by the dictionary and to sentences by the grammar correspond to things and their relations in reality. (4) So that process in reality has the nature of a sentence or sequence of sentences. (5) And that time correspondingly unfolds itself in the grammatical order of a sequence of sentences. (6) That orderly narration faithfully represents how things happen. (7) That history, whether 'real' or fictive, reveals its truth, if any, only to literary procedures that stress the representation of (*a*) abstraction, (*b*) chronological sequence, (*c*) causal sequence, and (*d*) identity of persons. (8) That the ideal for thought is to remain outside what it thinks about, and consequently to treat its subject matter as a concluded whole.

But in *Finnegans Wake* it is inescapable that language is a bodily thing, having to do somewhat intimately with thought, true, but always as thought by or through the medium of a bodily instrument that is spitting, sputtering, coughing, sneezing, braying, howling, chuckling, clearing itself, and saying 'um' between words. It is salutary, if humbling, to be made to consider how very many things we do with the voice other than, as we proudly say, 'make sense.' In this connection I note that Joyce's distortion of words is not always meant to secure a multiplicity of meanings; not infrequently it seems to reach out deliberately for the subhuman, and for the dissolution of meaning entirely for a moment (when I suggested earlier that the method might be easy to adapt for other writers I didn't mean this part of it).

Moreover, because all this is happening in a dream there is a further inference to be drawn from the emphasis on the bodily nature of language: whatever the overt subject, with all its ambiguities, may be, the language is liable to be thinking, or enacting, the body's sleep at the same time—the sweatings, the pricklings, the rumbling in the bowels; and some of the most genial comedy of the book comes, too, from the circumstance that at all times the most learned language is but a step from a fart or a snore.

Now I may not think that this circumstance is always a blessing. And on the whole I am just as pleased that Joyce's method has not been widely adapted by novelists, for instance, or by students writing term papers. Not only is it all too easy these days to blacken the character of 'the still and mental parts'; there's also this, that when the Joycean language fails of genius, and it does even in the hands of genius—when it fails to be genial, it hits the abyss without interval; there's no middle way.

Still, I shall go on, though maybe only a little at a time. What a marvelous book! I even want to find out what happens over again next. And there's a wondrous helpful thing about reading a book you know you don't understand; it may teach you something about all those other books you thought you did.

Part Three

WHAT WAS MODERN POETRY?
THREE LECTURES

✤ ୕୬ᝅୖ ☙

I. *Image and Metaphor*

When you look back on what is called Modern Poetry in the light of the assumption that it is now over, its victories won for good and ill, its spirit accepted as the very ground of our thoughts and our feelings, the liberties from tradition it insisted on also accepted to the point of becoming matters of indifference, you discover a rather strange thing: you don't find it at all easy to remember what Modern Poetry was.

This is so, perhaps, because while something is visibly producing its manifestations all around you, so that you have no doubt of its existence, you incline to accept whatever fashionable name is commonly given, vaguely aware that the name contains contradictions that someone ought someday to resolve . . . but that is for the historians. Meanwhile you use the name and are confident of being understood; when the name 'Modern Poetry' comes up in a conversation devoted to examples of it, people rarely question the term itself, it is accepted in the way that people accept for convenience the name Time when they are asked What time is it? whereas when people ask themselves What is Time, the name itself is the first thing that comes into question.

There's this as well. If the name Modern Poetry is to become the historical shorthand label for a period of time, it will have to cover the poetry written during that period, which I should roughly limit as the poetry written during the first half of the present century, though I am aware that others would locate it more narrowly, 1910–1925 for instance, and that still others would say it was still going on. But one remembers that the term had its not inconsiderable liveliness in argument just because it distinguished itself from 'contemporary.' Robert Frost was contemporary with Eliot and Pound, but he was not for a long time admitted to be modern with them, though curiously the very same poems that looked merely contemporary in 1940 made Frost seem a modern poet in 1960. Perhaps that is merely the snobbery that is compelled at last to include in its canon whatever has made great reputation, even if that reputation had to be made outside and indeed against the judgment of professionals in the first place.

You can see this clearly if you look for a moment at what would seem to be the most obvious characteristic of work that called itself Modern, its insistence on freedom from conventional forms. The supposed simplicity and purity of this distinction dissolve in endless nigglings and redefinitions, the plain fact of the matter being that despite all the noise made on the subject it was possible for poets to be accepted as Modern Poets whether they wrote free verse or whether they wrote sonnets, or whether they wrote both at once or in turn. If you look chiefly at manifestos and statements of intention, the question of free verse as over against conventional measure and form appears to be thematic for the entire period; but if you look at the poems you see that as a means of telling you who is a Modern Poet and who is not it is utterly confusing and indeterminate; it is rather like tracing the scatterings and involutions of typography in a poem by cummings only to find it is a sonnet.

There are, I think, thematic and recurrent questions raised in and by the poetry of the period, questions that are thematic for precisely the reason that they get answered in ever so many ways but never in such a way as to put the questions to rest; they come back. I make them out to be three in the main.

The first one centers on such questions as What is an image? When and how does it become a metaphor? Ought it to become a metaphor? At the extreme, some poets have tried to do without metaphor altogether, and some lines of critical thought have supplied, or attempted to supply, philosophical justification for this limitation, which seems to me a little like trying to walk on one foot; you might somehow justify it, for criticism can do much, but how can you do it? And other poets have tried to do without explicit or stated meaning.

The second theme has to do with the immense development of criticism, and especially interpretation, or instruction, during the century; so massive and energetic and programmatic a development as to suggest a shrewd definition of Modern Poetry: the poetry taught in universities.

My third theme is that of Myth, or—though it is best to say this in a low voice—Religion. I mean the often-heard-of obligation upon the

Modern Poet to invent, or revise, or somehow inherit all over again for the present century, an account of the creation in which poor old Modern Man—that allegorical invention who has forgotten what he is an allegory of—can invest the immense capital of his idle belief; to find him a god he will be able to pay lip service to.

I shall not here address each of these three themes. In this essay I shall simply try to show that the relation of image and meaning is both defining and difficult for Modern Poetry, to say something about the nature of the difficulties, and, with the help of some examples from William Carlos Williams, to indicate a few different ways of resolving those difficulties.

Poetry and Meaning

The simplest relation of image and meaning is assertive: Look at x, says the poet. I will describe it clearly, and then I will tell you what it means, at any rate what it is going to mean while it is in *my* poem. This is like the relation of photograph and caption. If it is so that the camera cannot lie, it must be so for the sufficient reason that the camera cannot tell the truth either: we look at a picture of a crowd, blurred whitish faces, blurred black clothing. Are they laughing? Praying? Watching a ball game? The caption tells us they are the survivors off a sunken ferry.

This relation of image and meaning is not only the plainest but also the least elegant and the least favored in modern times, yet it is the relation that obtains in a great deal of poetry, including, rather surprisingly, The Sonnets, many of which look as though Shakespeare wrote twelve lines and handed them to an apprentice—Here, boy, you've got two lines to say what this is all about. Modern readers are sometimes disappointed, not only because this relation of image and meaning is out of fashion but much more because Shakespeare's way of handling image, metaphor, and meaning in The Plays is one of the strongest reasons for the simpler relation's being out of fashion. Perhaps one way of accounting for the difference is overlooked: in The Plays the development of the plot and the behavior of the persons in relation to it steadily provide a rough approximation of meaning for the most complex figures in the verse, even in passages corrupt beyond emendation, such as Hamlet on the dram of eale and Othello on the green-eyed monster. In the context of speech and action the phrases are so clear and striking as to have become proverbs, though in strictness they have no assignable meaning. But in The Sonnets, meaning is rather baldly asserted, and the very form of the Shakespearian sonnet seems designed with this in view.

Dante, the complexity of whose poetic theory no one will dispute who has looked at the letter dedicating the *Paradiso* to Can Grande, nevertheless is quite firm on the plain separability of figure and meaning at least in the poet's mind: it would be a great shame, he says, for anyone to hide his subject under the clothing of metaphor or the colorings of rhetoric, and not be able later on to demand to strip his words of these garments in such a way as to produce a true understanding (*Vita Nuova*, XXV). Closely attended to, he seems to say that the meaning need not be supplied *in the poem,* and yet that the poem must have a plain—and separable—meaning.

It is a major tenet of modernism in literature that in one way or another—and I shall soon inspect examples of the ways—this assertive relation of image and meaning can be avoided and must at all costs be avoided. The cost is sometimes high indeed, and I find myself wondering if the progress of our explorations may not lead us round in a circle and back after all to the picture and the caption. But we shall see about that later. For the present I shall begin with the hypothesis that what modernism in writing is chiefly about is *seeing,* seeing as superior to thinking, as opposed to thinking, and something the poet must do instead of thinking if necessary. One notes already the suspicion of a difficulty, that all this affirmation of the eye at the mind's expense is an operation carried out and a decision taken by the mind, not by the eye. Nevertheless, this aspect of the Modern seems to be present about equally in the program of The Imagists, in Eliot's 'objective correlative,' in Joyce's 'epiphany' and in Hemingway's insistence on 'the way it was.' It is what Conrad believed about his art: 'It is above all in the first place to make you see.' One of the most celebrated recent definitions, or slogans, occurs in a little poem by William Carlos Williams, called 'A Sort of a Song.' I give it entire, though it is the second stanza I am chiefly concerned about.

A SORT OF A SONG

Let the snake wait under
his weed
and the writing

> *be of words, slow and quick, sharp*
> *to strike, quiet to wait,*
> *sleepless.*

> *—through metaphor to reconcile*
> *the people and the stones.*
> *Compose. (No ideas*
> *but in things) Invent!*
> *Saxifrage is my flower that splits*
> *the rocks.*

This little piece, whose enthusiastic assertiveness contrasts so oddly with the diffidence of its title, looks to be a very fair sample of a modernist poem, of the claims of modernist poetry in general, and of some of the difficulties the program imposes on the poems. I shall try to tell you some of the ways in which I think it is characteristic of a large and definite part of the mixed bag that gets labeled Modern Poetry.

First I observe that there is no point in saying it is written in free verse, for someone of the opposed persuasion would point out that it comes in two six-line stanzas; and if I objected that the stanzas didn't really match and indeed weren't really stanzas, he might bring in Dr. Williams's notion of the 'variable foot,' which is allowed to vary from one to ten syllables, leaving me speechless. The only thing the idea of free verse does for us here is to tell us that we have become free with respect to definitions and minimal with respect to forms.

The poem is about poetry, and this too is very modern, this reflexiveness. It has always been a possibility for poetry, but never so exploited as in the present century. There has even been collected a fine anthology of poems on poetry, and the flap copy gives me the information I should otherwise have had to spend an hour counting up for myself: of nearly 250 poems by 121 poets chosen from all periods and going as far back as the fourteenth century, half are by twentieth-century poets. One of the things this preoccupation of poetry with itself has seemed to me to mean is the end of poetry; but of that in another place.

The poem is about poetry, and wants to say what poetry ought to be, how poetry ought to go, and must be meant for an example of what it asserts on the subject. The first stanza says that writing, good writing presumably, should resemble a snake in being both slow and quick, sharp and quiet, sleepless. The second stanza offers more abstractly a program for poetry which involves imagism (no ideas but in things) but goes beyond imagism in having for its object

> *through metaphor to reconcile*
> *the people and the stones.*

The climactic image, though less reconciling about stones—of people nothing is said—is a happy one, and yet so narrowly or marginally so as to look a bit like special pleading. For a man to say in one breath 'no ideas but in things' and in the next to give saxifrage as his example is to triumph, but at some cost. Saxifrage is a good example for the excellent reason that its idea does happen to be in its name, which is Latin for *rock-breaker*.

And here is the main difficulty that imagism and its derivatives and variations run into every time. Most ideas are not contained in the mere names of things, nor even in the description of things, and have to be supplied from elsewhere. If you are and say you are in principle against any ideas save such as come packaged in things and the names of things, you will have to bootleg your ideas in somehow-anyhow and spatchcock them onto your poem somehow-anyhow, while continuing to proclaim you are doing no such thing. And that is what happens here.

Moreover, even in the fortunate choice of saxifrage—asphodel would not have done nearly so well in this poem, though it served the poet splendidly in a much better one—Dr. Williams is not at all content to let the idea arise from the thing; instead, he explains that saxifrage is a flower that splits the rocks. To be consistent with theory and program he should have ended the poem simply with the flower's name; and to be consistent with other of his views on an indigenous American poetry he should have said plainly: Sassafras.

Dr. Williams was on occasion a marvelous poet, and I shall come back to a few of his works to exemplify not only the difficulties of imagism but also, in one instance at least, the triumphant resolution of these. As to the present example, however, I will add that one can love a poet without being either cajoled or bulldozed into believing his theories. In fact, one of the hardest things about studying Modern Poetry is that you can write a far more coherent and plausible account from what the poets said they were doing than from their poems. This difficulty is compounded when the poems keep talking about themselves and their intentions for poetry as a whole.

The trouble with 'no ideas but in things' is much the same as the trouble with an earlier attempt of a similar sort, Archibald MacLeish's celebrated 'Ars Poetica,' with its slogan 'a poem should not mean but be'. As one of his exempla the poet gives us this image:

> *An empty doorway and a maple leaf,*

which we might either be puzzled by or so bemused by that we spend a long time listening to its reverberations in memory—except that he has prefaced the image by telling us it stands 'for all the history of grief.' The picture and the caption again, even if the caption has come first. Eliot assigned explicit meaning a low enough value for poetry when he compared it to a piece of meat that a burglar carries to quiet the watchdog; he did not suggest that burglars were likely to succeed better without such a sop. Yet something very like that, doing without meaning altogether, is what pure imagist theory demands, so that one consequence of pure imagist theory is that there could not be a pure imagist poem because it could not be as long as a line, else you would find you were talking about the object instead of presenting its image. Pound saw this when he defined an Image as 'that which presents an intellectual and emotional complex *in an instant of time.'* (My italics.) And he faced its extremest consequences: 'It is better to present one Image in a lifetime than to produce voluminous works.' After which he sat down to write the *Cantos.* Before doing so, however, he produced the example most often cited as the triumph of imagism, 'In a Station of the Metro.'

> *The apparition of these faces in the crowd;*
> *Petals on a wet, black bough.*

But in fact this is not an imagist poem at all, it is the statement of a relation, or what is traditionally called a metaphor, and as such suggests that the way out of the impasse offered by imagist programs is really the way back, modified by a few precepts such as Pound's insistence on 'Direct treatment of the "thing" whether subjective or objective,' his 'the natural object is always the *adequate* symbol,' and so on, some of them excellent instructions to keep tacked on the workshop wall but in no way remarkable for theory.

One striking thing about modernism in literature is its recurring or even nagging worry about diction, or what Henry James called 'rendering.' How to perceive, how to represent perception in language, how one's representations may rise into meaning and through meaning, one hopes, into revelation, all this is critical for the modern poet and suggests one affinity at least with the Romantics. Eliot shows it particularly by devoting one section of each Quartet to the struggle with language; Pound returns to it over and over; Wallace Stevens, one might say without greatly exaggerating, made it his subject matter. It is an aspect of that reflexiveness of poetry in this age that I spoke of before. But instead of appealing to poems that discuss themselves explicitly, I shall try to illustrate the problem of representation and meaning by three poems of William Carlos Williams that go about resolving that problem in three distinct ways.

YOUNG SYCAMORE

I must tell you
this young tree
whose round and firm trunk
between the wet

pavement and the gutter
(where water
is trickling) rises
bodily

into the air with
one undulant
thrust half its height—
and then

dividing and waning
sending out
young branches on
all sides—

hung with cocoons
it thins
till nothing is left of it
but two

eccentric knotted
twigs
bending forward
hornlike at the top

Williams wrote a good many poems of this somewhat noncommital sort, poems that say in effect scarcely more than Look! you must look, or, in this instance 'I must tell you.' They appear to me as expressing, on the negative side, a fear that not only the secondary imagination, the one that writes poems, but the primary one, which gives us the world instead of a congeries of electro-chemical and sense-specific stimuli, is in serious likelihood of being lost—perhaps by being geometrized and climate-controlled out of existence as the world tends to become ever more like a city or an airport. I chose this example out of many, however, because a spirited and in many ways illuminating defense of it has been written by J. Hillis Miller in the Introduction to a volume of essays on Williams which he edited (*William Carlos Williams* [New York: Prentice Hall, 1966]).

I do not have space to do justice to the force of Professor Miller's argument, which you should read entire if the question continues to interest you. And though I shy away from the general conclusions as to poetic purpose to which it seems to lead, I am unable to refute it on its own grounds; I shall have to resort to a craven retreat upon differences of temperament and taste, maintaining sadly that 'Young Sycamore' continues to seem unremarkable to me even after Professor Miller's justifications. What these are I must now indicate as briefly and as clearly as I can.

We fail to respond to this poem, he says, because we come at it with traditional presuppositions related to Romanticism in the first place, and to the Christian and Platonic traditions to which Romanticism appeals for justification. In these traditions, 'things of this world in one way or another stand for things of the other world.' But 'in Williams's poetry this kind of depth has disappeared and with it the symbolism appropriate to it.'

> There can also be for Williams little figurative language, little of that creation of a 'pattern of imagery' which often unifies poems written in older traditions. Metaphors compare one thing to another and so blur the individuality of those things. For

Williams the uniqueness of each thing is more important than any horizontal resonances it may have with other things.

Again,

Romantic and symbolist poetry is usually an art of willed transformation. In this it is, like science or technology, an example of that changing of things into artifacts which assimilates them into the human world. Williams's poetry, on the other hand, is content to let things be. A good poet, he says, 'doesn't *select* his material. What is there to select? It *is*.'

Such a poem, says Miller, 'seems recalcitrant to analysis. The sycamore is not a symbol.' And he recurs to this thought, expressing it a bit more fully as well as, one thinks, with a touch of quiet desperation, a couple of pages later:

No symbolism, no depth, no reference to a world beyond the world, no pattern of imagery, no dialectical structure, no interaction of subject and object—just description. How can the critic 'analyze' such a poem? What does it mean? Of what use is it?

One realizes, seeing that the critic has six or seven pages still to go, that this is part of the drama. Moreover, he has already said that what Williams is up to in this as in each of his poems 'can only be discovered by that immersion in his writing which must precede interpretation of any part of it.' This is a sound maxim for the scholar, though a person accustomed to now and then reading a poem and maybe liking it may feel a touch put off by its austerity.

For Miller, the representative anecdote of Williams's poetics is an early poem, 'The Wanderer,' which 'ends with the protagonist's plunge into "the filthy Passaic." He is swallowed up by "the utter depth of its rottenness" until his separate existence is lost, and he can say, "I knew it all—it became me."' And he quotes from a letter the poet wrote to Marianne Moore about '"A sort of nameless religious experience," "a despair which made everything a unit and at the same time a part of myself."' That fall into the river, that resignation to being one with the river and its filth as a means to knowledge, Miller suggests, is at the basis of Williams's mature poetry, in which 'there is no description of private inner experience' and 'no description of objects which are external to the poet's mind. Nothing is external to his mind.'

There is a good deal more, but I had better limit myself to quoting the most concentrated passage of particular interpretation I can find:

> A grammatical peculiarity of the poem may be noted here as a stroke of genius which makes the poem a perfect imitation of the activity of nature. When the undulant thrust from trunk to twigs has been followed to its end the sycamore seems to stand fixed, its energy exhausted, the vitality which urged it into the air now too far from its source in the dark earth. But this is not really true. The inexhaustible force of the temporal thrust of the tree is expressed not only in the cocoons which promise a renewal of the cycle of growth, but also in the fact that there is no main verb in the second clause of the long sentence which makes up the poem. The poem contains so much verbal action that this may not be noticed, but all these verbs are part of a subordinate clause following 'whose.' Their subject is 'trunk' not 'tree,' and 'trunk' is also the apparent referent of 'it' in line eighteen. All the movement in the poem takes place within the confines of the subordinate clause. The second line, 'this young tree,' still hovers incomplete at the end of the poem, reaching out toward the verb which will complement its substantiality with an appropriate action. If the subordinate clause is omitted the poem says: 'I must tell you this young tree'—and then stops. This is undoubtedly the way the poet wanted it. It makes the poem hold permanently open that beauty which is revealed in the tree. . . .

And one more passage in summation:

> Here is a concept of poetry which differs both from the classical theory of art as a mirror held up to nature and from the romantic theory of art as a lamp radiating unifying light. The word is given reality by the fact it names, but the independence of the fact from the word frees the word to be a fact in its own right and at the same time 'dynamizes' it with meaning. The word can then carry the facts named in a new form into the realm of imagination. In this sense poetry rescues and completes. It lifts things up . . . as the words are liberated, so are the facts they name. . . .

O dear, it feels very strange to be quoting all this at you when I don't seem to understand it at all well myself . . . especially that last passage, which seems to me written in the lofty language of Art Criticism. But I suppose that if you care for the poem the interpreter's dry enthusiasm over missing verbs and the like will perhaps be your enthusiasm also.

Nevertheless it seems right to have given Hillis Miller's argument for the poem and its principles a fairly full account, for it is an argument much heard of these days. A near equivalent for fiction is Alain Robbe-Grillet's essay 'Toward a New Fiction,' though there, oddly enough, the rejection of metaphor—and on the basis of such examples as 'the village *crouching* at the mountain's foot,' yet—is said to lead, not to oneness with things, but precisely to separation and distance from things. It's a hard game, the art game, where they change the rules before you half get started. Some bright fellow once said this in a somewhat more sparkling manner: the artist, he said, is like the crooked gambler who turns up with his marked cards and loaded dice only to find he is entered in the six-day bike race; he will be breathless before he can rest on the seventh day.

But onward.

My second example is of a kind quite rare in Williams's work, for it represents him as trying to come to terms with traditional values of verse and construction that for the most part he rejected, often violently; yet it seems to me a beautiful poem.

THE YACHTS

contend in a sea which the land partly encloses
shielding them from the too-heavy blows
of an ungoverned ocean which when it chooses

tortures the biggest hulls, the best man knows
to pit against its beatings, and sinks them pitilessly.
Mothlike in mists, scintillant in the minute

brilliance of cloudless days, with broad bellying sails
they glide to the wind tossing green water
from their sharp prows while over them the crew crawls

ant-like, solicitously grooming them, releasing,
making fast as they turn, lean far over and having
caught the wind again, side by side, head for the mark.

In a well guarded arena of open water surrounded by
lesser and greater craft which, sycophant, lumbering
and flittering follow them, they appear youthful, rare

as the light of a happy eye, live with the grace

of all that in the mind is feckless, free and
naturally to be desired. Now the sea which holds them

is moody, lapping their glossy sides, as if feeling
for some slightest flaw but fails completely.
Today no race. Then the wind comes again. The yachts

move jockeying for a start, the signal is set and they
are off. Now the waves strike at them but they are too
well made, they slip through, though they take in canvas.

Arms with hands grasping seek to clutch at the prows.
Bodies thrown recklessly in the way are cut aside.
It is a sea of faces about them in agony, in despair

until the horror of the race dawns staggering the mind,
the whole sea become an entanglement of watery bodies
lost to the world bearing what they cannot hold. Broken,

beaten, desolate, reaching from the dead to be taken up
they cry out, failing, failing! their cries rising
in waves still as the skillful yachts pass over.

The verse hovers irregularly around a pentameter norm, but is not iambic; more likely its principle is alliterative, again irregularly so. You can see from the beginning that the poet may even have meant to cast the whole into *terza rima,* but by line five he is seen to abandon that idea, perhaps because the alliterative enters so powerfully with the punning resonance of 'pit.... pitilessly.' And in the next line he even becomes rhapsodic and as it were abandoned to lyricism to a degree unusual indeed in this poet of so resolute a plainness:

> *Mothlike in mists, scintillant in the minute*
> *brilliance of cloudless days....*

Later on you have the rhapsodic and climaxing release of energy in the series of comparisons in which the yachts

> *appear youthful, rare*

> *as the light of a happy eye, live with the grace*
> *of all that in the mind is feckless, free and*
> *naturally to be desired.*

Now the poem appears at a first reading to divide rather simply into description, in the first eight tercets, and meaning, or moral, in the last three. The picture and the caption again, although we may be surprised and even a little chagrined at seeing so grim a caption under so pretty a picture. If that is the best Williams can do with tradition, we may think, he was quite right to abandon tradition and do something else. Or if that is indeed what the tradition looks like, we had better agree to abandon it ourselves.

But if now, knowing what the poet will assert at the end, we go back and inspect his poem more attentively than at first we shall see, I think, that the picture and caption idea will not cover his procedures. For what the concluding passages of explicit prophetic fury and denunciation say so plainly has been developing from the beginning, making it clear that the poem is metaphysical and emblematic, working on the principle of metaphor that says: What men do is the visible sign of what they are.

It is not so much that yachts and yacht-racing form an allegory of the workings of society, in this instance a society based upon free enterprise capitalism, but that these institutions and their associated imagery are in themselves the making visible of the beauty and the horror of a competition claimed to be held under the laws of nature but where the laws of nature are rigged in favor of great wealth.

Consider if that not be the meaning of the first thing we are told, that the yacht race is not held out in the open water where the yachts would be exposed to the force of 'an ungoverned ocean' too great for them. The same idea returns, with a more overt sarcasm, in 'a well guarded arena of open water,' which invites us to read an equivocation in the 'lesser and greater craft' of the following line. It is not necessary to make explicit the equation: yachts are, say, business enterprises, family fortunes. They are yachts, and what is said of them applies to yachts and yacht-racing; nevertheless what is said of them makes them stand forth as symbolic of certain characteristics of the marketplace from which they come.

And then with superb outrage the poet throws aside the veil of the visible as he sees it will no longer satisfy the demands of his figure. The figure, rather, works for the undeniable beauty of the scene, which is a part of the paradox that makes the poem tragic. But the boats with their sharp prows cutting the waters have by now developed by the poet's perception of them into a further metaphor representing the pitiless and unequal warfare carried on by the rich against the poor. To be 'live with the grace of all that in the mind is feckless, free and naturally to be desired' requires, alas, this cruel corollary, that it can be done only by those who inflict massive sufferings on others and who remain massively indifferent to these sufferings.

It is not, I should say, the moral of the poem that makes it a success, but rather the process whereby first the poet and now his readers come to perceive a developing relation. The perception is at first implicit in natural things, by the language employed to tell of them, which cannot rid itself of an insistent undertone of symbolism that finally breaks openly into revelation.

In my view, 'The Yachts' is a superior poem to 'Young Sycamore.' But I feel uncomfortably as if Hillis Miller may be right about the premises upon which I base my preference; tersely, that I can 'do more' with the one poem than with the other, and that this about doing more with a poem reflects the fact that I am a teacher, defined by Ezra Pound as a man who must talk for an hour. In a social situation where the appropriate response to poetry was to keep quiet in its presence my liking might go the other way, and I might prefer the poem that has, so to say, nothing behind it, nothing underlying, no 'depth,' but simply is. People who do not much care for 'The Yachts,' or for the sort of traditional enterprise I find it to represent, might easily enough condescend to it by calling it a rationally appreciable schoolroom good poem, a description which they would easily enough condense to calling it worthless. Indeed, I myself do not think 'The Yachts' either representative of Williams's work in poetry or an instance of Williams at his best; I chose it because it is uncharacteristic and therefore, I hope, illuminating about our general question of the relation of image and meaning.

So to finish up with, here is a poem by Williams that for me is a masterpiece, and about as far superior to 'The Yachts' as I believe that poem is to 'Young Sycamore.'

THE SEMBLABLES

The red brick monastery in
the suburbs over against the dust-
hung acreage of the unfinished
and all but subterranean

munitions plant: those high
brick walls behind which at Easter
the little orphans and bastards
in white gowns sing their Latin

responses to the hoary ritual
while frankincense and myrrh
round out the dark chapel making
an enclosed sphere of it

of which they are the worm:
that cell outside the city beside
the polluted stream and dump
heap, uncomplaining, and the field

of upended stones with a photo
under glass fastened here and there
to one of them near the deeply
carved name to distinguish it:

that trinity of slate gables
the unembellished windows piling
up, the chapel with its round
window between the dormitories

peaked by the bronze belfry
peaked in turn by the cross,
verdegris—faces all silent
that miracle that has burst sexless

from between the carrot rows.
Leafless white birches, their
empty tendrils swaying in
the all but no breeze guard

behind the spiked monastery fence
the sacred statuary. But ranks
of brilliant car-tops row on row
give back in all his glory the

late November sun and hushed
attend, before that tumbled
ground, those sightless walls
and shovelled entrances where no

one but a lonesome cop swinging
his club gives sign, that agony
within where the wrapt machines
are praying. . . .

Now this is in no way the rationally appreciable schoolroom good; it is, to me at least, beautiful with that mysterious beauty that only high art can make arise from sorrow, pity, horror, ugliness itself. For the most part as casual, low-keyed, and 'objective' as 'Young Sycamore,' it seems to represent only such architecture as one might naturally encounter while walking around just at the edge of town. The notation is spare and not insistent, unemotional except for one sardonic comment near the beginning and the breaking forth of the hitherto suppressed feeling in 'that agony' at the end. Yet it is all metaphor, all relation, and working throughout on that principle of metaphor I mentioned earlier, that what men do—the buildings they build, for instance—is the making visible of what they are. The poem says almost nothing aloud, limiting itself to rather bare description, yet idea is everywhere radiantly present. These buildings are put together—*composed*—in the poem, one feels, because that is the way they are put together in the world. The relations among them—munitions plant, orphanage, monastery, cemetery—silently *are* the relations that compose this hopeless, hideous world; and yet, in that strange and decisive image of the brilliant car-tops seen as worshippers of some sacred and doubtless horrifying principle enshrined in the munitions plant, everything— without in the least denying the horror and the hideousness—becomes beautiful.

Something like that, I think, is what imagism must always have meant but almost never done. It is, in the hands of a master of our time, a property of poetry that was scarcely available to earlier poetry with its more explicit—and perhaps less adventurous—attachment to meaning. For in 'The Semblables,' meaning—in the form at first only of relation—appears to arise from the collocation of things all by itself. The poem shows what can be done by a humble and accurate attention to the things of the world in their places in the world; it is the product of what I shall call, paradoxically, a disinterested passion, a love that is able to let go, maybe even a love of letting go. Its program is eloquently set forth by another master of the present time, Pablo Neruda:

It is well, at certain hours of the day and night, to look closely at the world of objects at rest. Wheels that have crossed long, dusty distances with their mineral and vegetable burdens, sacks from the coalbins, barrels and baskets, handles and hafts for the carpenter's tool chest. From them flow the contacts of man with the earth, like a text for all harassed lyricists. The used surfaces of things, the wear that the hands give to things, the air, tragic at times, pathetic at others, of such things—all lend a curious attractiveness to the reality of the world that should not be underprized.

In Dr. Williams's homelier diction, it is indeed

through metaphor to reconcile
the people and the stones.

II. *Poetry and History*

In my first lecture, I spent almost all the time on what I called imagism—not the movement called Des Imagistes, but, much more broadly, the many and recurrent movements in modernist poetry that had in common a wish to exalt the senses, especially the sense of sight at the expense of the mind. Indeed, these movements, like some movements in philosophy (and not in the branch of aesthetics alone), found themselves impelled, by the necessities of rhetoric if by nothing more serious, to a contempt for mind, and since this contempt for mind in general had to include of necessity the mind that was being contemptuous, not to mention the mind that was writing the poems that exalted the senses at the mind's expense, some contradiction was always involved, though it was not always acknowledged. For to proclaim, as the first Imagists did, that one must do away with 'Cosmic Poetry' is to proclaim that one must do away with metaphysics, which is, however, a metaphysical decision; and as Owen Barfield says, 'It is a failing common to a good many contemporary metaphysical theories that they can be applied to all things except themselves but that, when so applied, they extinguish themselves' (*Poetic Diction* [New York: McGraw-Hill, 1964], p. 16).

Having tried to illustrate by certain poems of William Carlos Williams what theoretical considerations, what problems, and what solutions belonged to this movement of the mind, I wish now to ask why. Why should it have happened to so many talented men and women, in poetry, in the novel, not to mention in painting, to put such an exclusive emphasis upon sensing, so exclusive that it led them in many instances to a contemptuous or fierce rejection of mind and thinking and explicitly stated meaning? One would have thought there could never have been a poet or novelist or painter so foolish as to be *against* accuracy of perception, accuracy of notation, or *against* the sympathetic concentration upon nature which alone could enable such accuracy—but why was it, why is it, this stress on seeing, almost always as if of necessity accompanied by an assault on the still and mental parts?

I remind you of some of the forms this twinned attitude took during the early part of the period, where the stress is upon immediacy of experience either in neglect of reason or more often in denial or contradiction of reason. Eliot, who gave us the 'objective correlative,' also praised Donne because his thought was as immediate to him as the odor of a rose. Hopkins, whose visionary contemplation of divinity both in and behind nature proceeded by an 'instress' in the self that corresponded with an 'inscape' in the object, made an appealing slogan for his procedures: What you look hard at seems to look hard at you. D. H. Lawrence interested himself fiercely in a relation to the universe that should proceed directly to and from the genitals and the solar plexus, omitting as entirely as might be the brain he thought responsible for the world's damage; he wanted, poetically and piously, to see process instead of result—'the perfect rose is only a running flame,' he said—and cursed the mind with all his mind. Even Proust in his great work yields an example of this strange contradiction: a man patiently and laboriously researching the past in minutest detail, and constructing by the habit of the hardest daily work a book whose two main principles are that voluntary memory is futile and that habit prevents us from seeing truly. Many more instances, among the great and the not-so-great, will occur to you. But I must now try to say why it was so.

My answer is a hypothesis, and it can take form both simple and complex. Most simply: history was—and still is—becoming elusive as well as ever more uncomfortable. Poets and novelists are people whose vocation it is to see and say as much as possible the whole of things rather than their division into categories; they are sensitive to a wholeness they believe to be really there and really prepotent over appear-

ances even if it can be grasped only by synoptic and symbolic vision
attending to minute particulars.

When one tries to specify a little more this elusiveness of history, the
same hypothesis takes a more complicated, more problematic, maybe
even a more dubious form. This form has to do with the amazing
growth of the scientific way of viewing the world, and with the corresponding growth of the technological way of changing the world that
went along with it. Most plainly, the poets have never been happy
under the reign of Newtonian mechanics and Kantian criticism. Their
distrust of, their protests against, the consequences entailed upon life
and thought by this physics and this philosophy form a major strand in
the movement known as Romanticism, which indeed may not be over
yet. For it was the effect of Newton to remove mind from the cosmos
except as a passive recording instrument, and the effect of the domi-
nance of Kant's philosophy to remove from remaining mind any access
whatever to ultimate reality. Whereas poetic thought can proceed beyond the minimal affirmation of parlor verse only upon the supposition
that the world is equally and simultaneously perceivable as real and as
transpicuous, or sacramental, and that no percept is ever divorced
entirely from concept. Poetic thought is indeed in this respect primitive, though its primitivism may take highly sophisticated forms; and
it is beautifully described by Claude Lévi-Strauss in talking about
savage thought, 'definable,' he says, 'both by a consuming symbolic
ambition such as humanity has never again seen rivalled, and by scru-
pulous attention directed entirely toward the concrete, and finally by
the implicit conviction that these two attitudes are one.' A page earlier,
indeed, he makes the parallel in a piquant and illuminating way:
'Whether one deplores or rejoices in the fact, there are still zones in
which savage thought, like savage species, is relatively protected. This
is the case of art, to which our civilization accords the status of a
national park, with all the advantages and inconveniences attending so
artificial a formula' (*The Savage Mind* [Chicago: The University of
Chicago Press, 1967], pp. 220, 219).

I am neither historian nor philosopher, and this is not the occasion
for a philosophical discourse or one on the history of mind. One proposition that follows from my hypothesis is that imagism in its varieties
arose as one response of the imagination to a development that saw
mind—often by the hardest thought—progressively being read out of
the universe along with gods, devils, spirits, the spirit, and so much
else. As I tried to show in the first lecture, imagism seems to me a

crippled and crippling response, though it has its rare triumphs; what it amounts to is abandoning what has been lost and making costume jewelry of the little that remains; and its ultimate effect is in a sense on the side of technology, as poetry becomes simply one more specialization. A linguistic philosopher said to me, in the course not of trying to convert me but of showing that I was in fact already one of the happy flock, 'You could still write your poetry, so long as you were quite clear it was... poetry.' Where he paused I silently supplied the word 'only,' and I don't think I was in error to do so.

What I hope to do in this chapter is to discuss examples of other kinds of poetic response to the question of history. For reasons of time, though, as well as for the prevention of tedium, I am not going to bother with the biggest examples, which have in common not only their size and other things formidable about them but also the fact that they are extremely well-known to all who do not read them; I mean the *Cantos, Paterson, The Dynasts, Finnegans Wake, The Anathemata, ...* even *The Waste Land,* whose compactness allows it to be read even though it is in other respects comparable to the works I have named, is not to my purpose, for it has been too much discussed. Instead, I shall use smaller and more compassable examples, short poems that appear to me to grow from within, by the reader's meditation upon them, rather than by accretions and additions from without.

Before presenting my examples, however, I should say a word or so about science, for it is very likely that some of you will accuse me of being against it. And so far as a somewhat called *science* can be isolated for inspection—and that is fairly far—I should feel sorry, as well as look silly, to be thought against something so massively and so brilliantly present and part of reality; anyhow, it would be unbecoming for anyone to stand in an air-conditioned room and say mean things about science through a microphone.

But owing to that sense of wholeness I spoke of earlier, the poets whose poems I have chosen to bring evidence for my hypothesis do not separate out, at least in their poems, a somewhat called science to be for or against. They seem to me to be looking at, and trying to phrase in the lightning instant of their figured speech, as much as possible of what happened in the world since, say, the Renaissance. What they see is terrible, and what they say ranges from the neutrally diagnostic to prophetic sorrow and prophetic rage, but it is not, I think, against science, if only for the reason that in poetic thought science cannot stand alone but must be taken along with many other forces and their results. There may be much gold, the poets seem to say, though even of that we are sometimes doubtful; but you will be plain foolish if you pretend that the gold is not guarded by a dragon, or if you pretend that the gold is real and the dragon is not. *Satis quod sufficit.*

Yeats included in *The Tower* (1928) a poem of two parts to which he gave the unusual, hence suggestive, title of 'Fragments.' The first of these fragments may stand as a text to any sermon I might give on the relations among modern poetry, modern science, and modern history:

I

Locke sank into a swoon;
The Garden died;
God took the spinning-jenny
Out of his side.

There it is, a four-line creation myth, possibly the shortest one ever made. The second fragment does nothing to make our way easier, but we ought to have it before us anyhow:

I I

Where got I that truth?
Out of a medium's mouth,
Out of nothing it came,
Out of the forest loam,
Out of dark night where lay
The crowns of Nineveh.

Nineveh was characterized by the Lord in a rare flash of sardonic humor: 'that great city, wherein are more than sixscore thousand persons that cannot discern between their right hand and their left hand; and also much cattle' (Jonah 4:11). It might be a type of modern metropolis.

John Locke, English philosopher, lived in the seventeenth century. He is remembered chiefly for *An Essay Concerning Human Understanding,* and what we chiefly remember about that essay, I think, and what makes Locke appropriate to Yeats's myth, is his separation of primary from secondary qualities, the primary ones being present in the object as in our experience of it, the secondary ones, such as smell and color, being in the object, if at all, in some mode other than the mode in which they are experienced by the senses. It was a momentous separation, and a step on the way to the curiously contradictory attitude of modern science and Kantian philosophy toward the senses, simultaneously relying on and discrediting their evidences. I think it is this separation, leading on to that all too well-known modern division of subjective and objective, that Yeats has in mind in rewriting the creation of woman as it is told in the second chapter of Genesis.

The spinning-jenny, the first machine for making wool or cotton into thread, and said to be the prototype for mass production, may be taken as a synecdoche for the Industrial Revolution generally but it has some special appropriatenesses of its own. One is, of course, that it is a girl's name, another is that it echoes 'Genesis,' from whose root it may ultimately have derived, and a third, perhaps more compelling still, is that the Fall of Adam and Eve (or Locke and the spinning-jenny) from innocence to guilt is specifically marked by their awakening to shame over their nakedness and their consequent haste to make themselves aprons, or, as one translation said, breeches. Which may be why we now wear underpants labeled Fruit of the Loom. Had Yeats had that happy conceit to hand, might he have written 'Fragments, III'?

> *The Mechanical Bride, McLuhan said;*
> *And now the access to the womb,*
> *The path that leads among the dead,*
> *Hides in the cotton fruit of the loom.*

Maybe. But notice anyhow that while everyone nowadays knows all about McLuhan, not to mention sex and birth and death, readers unprovided with the right underwear would find the poem obscure, perhaps impenetrably so.

Having got so far as that, I stopped for a few days; for the immediate if trivial reason that the book from which I wanted to quote my second example was several miles away. But while I stopped I began to think, and everyone knows that is injurious to a writer. What I began to think about was myth and truth, and what one of this pair had a right to demand of the other. I said that Yeats's witty and elegant four lines made a creation myth; by correspondence with the story of the birth of Eve, and by making us think of the consequences of that birth and of this, he is giving us one version of how the modern world, so different from the other one, came into being. And I suppose now that what stopped me, apart from the missing book, were two related questions:

What does this myth tell me about the emergence of the modern world? and Do I believe it? At the risk of running off the planned path of this essay altogether, it seems to me that I ought to consider these questions for a little while. I do not believe so much as I formerly did in the efficacy of 'close reading,' or explication; I should far rather be able to take the little poem as a talisman, something to say over to oneself as though it meant something rather important, without inquiring too closely into what the importance might be. And yet it seems as if I should be leaving the account badly unfinished, did I not look more closely into what is going on.

'Locke sank into a swoon; The Garden died.'... Several things about this. Locke is, I suppose among the foremost of those philosophers who limited their account of human understanding to what went on in consciousness, to the daylight side, and who preferred judgment over wit, or as we should say, reason over imagination. He sank into a swoon. Compare Genesis 2.21. 'And the Lord God caused a deep sleep to fall upon Adam, and he slept.' And contrast Yeats's own and lovely line: 'When the bride-sleep fell upon Adam.' The first two lines may suggest, anticipating Berkeley, or rather, anticipating a common and erroneous reading of Berkeley, that the world of experience is sustained only by our attention (in the true reading, it is sustained by God's attention); an erroneous reading out of which Yeats made three splendidly eloquent lines:

> And God-appointed Berkeley that proved all things a dream,
> That this pragmatical, preposterous pig of a world, its farrow
>   that so solid seem,
> Must vanish on the instant if the mind but change its theme.

('Blood and the Moon,' II)

You can read the first two lines of fragment 1 in two opposed ways. Either the Garden died when and because Locke lost consciousness; or else Locke's sinking into a swoon is a sarcastic representation of Locke's conscious thought itself as tantamount to what Blake had called 'single vision and Newton's sleep.' Not only innocence was lost by the separation of primary and secondary qualities, in this myth; but the secondary qualities themselves, all the properties of things least amenable to measurement, what Hopkins would think of as the dapple and piedness of experience—all these were by that separation on the road to being lost, and the world, in consequence of Locke's kind of thought, was started on a course of mechanizing at first things and then peoples and the thoughts they had.

It is true that Yeats was resentful of science, as he was of democracy and trade and logic and a good many other what he thought of as leveling notions; in a much-quoted passage of his *Autobiographies* he speaks of being deprived of the simple-minded religion of his childhood 'by Huxley and Tyndall, whom I detested,' and of his making 'a new religion, almost an infallible church of poetic tradition, of a fardel of stories, and of personages, and of emotions, inseparable from their first expression, passed on from generation to generation of poets and painters with some help from philosophers and theologians' (*Autobiographies* [New York: Macmillan, 1938], p. 101). But this Fragment is not directed simply at science; rather, it involves in its grotesque parody of creation and fall a strange, indeed paradoxical, association of mind and matter. Both Fragments assert the primacy of myth over reason, of nothing over something; the second is like the first in being an account of how one kind of thing emerged out of another kind of thing; it suggests that even a thought must first be a picture, a story, and that this picture or story, this 'truth' as he calls it, does not proceed from reasoning at all, but comes first from a medium's mouth (matching the 'swoon' of the first fragment?), then, beyond that, from 'nothing,' up out of the 'forest loam,' 'Out of dark night where lay / The crowns of Nineveh.' And yet it is precisely these dark absences and emptinesses and swoons and trancelike sleeps that cause to arise the myth about a history in which machines are reasoned up out of the earth by the change in a philosopher's mind; for it seems pertinent to the history of the past few centuries to say that it is the history of mind producing, as the result of a striking new attitude toward its own experiences, machines which then become models for the mind and for thinking.

In some such way, says the myth, the world changed, and in Yeats's view it changed for the worse. The change was from a real or presumed fourfold unity of sense, thought, feeling, and intuition, giving rise to a fourfold unity of letter, allegory, moral, and anagoge, to 'single vision and Newton's sleep,' it was in the first place a change in vision, for as Blake saw and said in so many ways, 'You become what you behold,' and it produced the mental world that Blake characterized as 'the Loom of Locke, whose Woof rages dire, / Washed by the Water-wheels of Newton,' the world committed to think ever more on mechanical principles and by means of mechanical models at the spirit's expense. Yeats, who had edited the works of Blake and been among the first to heed *The Prophetic Books,* was much at home among such phrases as I have quoted, and in effect, in the 'Fragments' and elsewhere, he is taking up the song a century after Blake left it.

These reflections began more or less in the consciousness of their being digressive; yet now I think I can tie them up and even justify going a bit further with them, at the expense of what comment I might have made on my other examples. My subject, after all, is Poetry and History, and though Yeats was by no means alone among modern poets in addressing himself to the theme of historical change, and especially to what sort of change produced the world of the twentieth century, he held himself to this theme more consistently, and made his account of it more coherent, than most.

It is a striking thing about many of the intellectual heroes of the present age, that those of them that lived long were able to experience two quite different worlds; their childhood and youth were passed in the old world, their productive maturity and age in the new. In some instances, too, the new they experienced was the new they had in part themselves created. I think here especially of Einstein and Freud, but would also bring into this category the literary and artistic folk whose works are both diagnostic and prophetic of what I shall call The Great Change.

I hope to stress this point without overstressing it. No doubt history was present to the man of 1890 as to the man of 1920; or maybe not quite so present, not quite so immediate, not quite so overwhelming. And the world has always been a sufficiently terrible place for most of the people in it. Yet there did come The Great Change, and there is ample evidence of its having been experienced as such by the writers and artists that lived through it. The War of 1914–1918 in part *was* this great change, and in part was but the astounding revelation of its more continuous and subtle workings over a long time. History swallows so much so easily, that it may take a considerable effort of the mind for us to place ourselves in a situation so unprecedented as then confronted the most civilized intelligences of Europe. It seemed to Freud to reveal that 'the state has forbidden to the individual the practice of wrong-doing, not because it desired to abolish it, but because it desires to monopolize it, like salt and tobacco' ('Thoughts for the Times on War and Death,' 1915). And to Valéry, beginning an essay in 1919, the lesson was as clear as it was somber: 'We know now, we other civilizations, that we too are mortal.' The recent histories by Barbara Tuchman are most helpful on this theme, *The Guns of August* showing how utterly surprising and unforeseen were the events let loose upon 1914, even among those most responsible for the decisions immediately leading to them, *The Proud Tower* recording with picturesque charm and in much detail some of the ways in which Before was decisively different from After. In fiction, it is perhaps Ford Madox Ford's great tetralogy *No More Parades* that more than any other work will give us a sense of this incredible discontinuity in experience, and not more by the events it records than by the stylistic substitutions and dissolutions of the successive volumes.

Yeats's experience of the Great Change came in the first place more from Irish than from European history, from the Easter Rising of 1916 and from the Civil War that won Ireland its independence, however much he attempted poetically to generalize these events and to mythify them, later on, as elements in his necessitarian model for history. All the same, the shock in his poems reflecting upon this change is unmistakable: he is bewildered, even stupefied, perhaps bewildered and stupefied into becoming a great poet. The Fall of Man appears not only in the little gnomic epigram I have quoted, but in a number of the poems of the books following The Great War, and by bringing in evidence from some of these I may perhaps be able to make the myth about Locke and the spinning-jenny more richly unfold its inward workings.

What I have to show is speculative and must remain so, yet I hope it will seem a probable set of relations. For a poet, especially one who is productive over a long period and through the several stages of life's way, develops his own vocabulary, which though not necessarily in denial of meaning assigned the words in dictionaries is nevertheless not entirely confined to those meanings; especially in relation with one another his favorite terms develop extra and hidden relations.

The moral of Yeats's great meditation 'Nineteen Hundred and Nineteen' corresponds closely with one of Freud's conclusions in the essay I have already quoted from; Freud considers it 'a consolation': 'that our mortification and our grievous disillusionment regarding the uncivilized behavior of our world-compatriots in this war are shown to be unjustified. They were based on an illusion to which we had abandoned ourselves. In reality our fellow-citizens have not sunk so low as we feared, because they had never risen so high as we believed' ('Thoughts for the Times on War and Death,' 1915).

In the same way, for Yeats,

> *The night can sweat with terror as before*
> *We pieced our thoughts into philosophy,*
> *And planned to bring the world under a rule,*
> *Who are but weasels fighting in a hole.*

> ('Nineteen Hundred and Nine-
> teen,' I)

The same figure returns as a savage epigram in IV:

> *We, who seven years ago*
> *Talked of honour and of truth,*
> *Shriek with pleasure if we show*
> *The weasel's twist, the weasel's tooth.*

The main sense of the whole poem is not that man has fallen, so much as that his fall has now been made evident even to civilized and cultivated persons who unthinkingly may have believed otherwise, who may out of security have been permitted to think otherwise. Accordingly the tone of the poem is bitter exultation: not civilization only, but we also who believed in it, who relied on it, who reposed in it our utmost confidence, are fraudulent and always were. The loss of innocence becomes a kind of brutal blessing, the stringent and salutary awakening from an illusion, as the poet savages himself and his contemporaries for their naivety in never having realized how precarious, contingent, and uncertain were the certainties in which they lived. The emblems of these certainties are Athenian: 'An ancient image made of olive wood . . . Phidias' famous ivories / And all the golden grasshoppers and bees.' These are, in the beginning of the poem, 'ingenious lovely things' that had seemed immortal, 'Protected from the circle of the moon / That pitches common things about.' And yet they are gone. 'We too,' he continues:

> *We too had many pretty toys when young:*
> *A law indifferent to blame or praise,*
> *To bribe or threat; habits that made old wrong*
> *Melt down, as it were wax in the sun's rays;*
> *Public opinion ripening for so long*

> *We thought it would outlive all future days.*
> *O what fine thought we had because we thought*
> *That the worst rogues and rascals had died out.*

We ought to have known, the poem seems to say, that no work can stand; we ought to have known, for 'Man is in love and loves what vanishes, / What more is there to say?' And yet men never do know; the Athenians didn't know, and wouldn't have spoken of it if they did:

> *That country round*
> *None dared admit, if such a thought were his,*
> *Incendiary or bigot could be found*
> *To burn that stump on the Acropolis,*
> *Or break in bits the famous ivories*
> *Or traffic in the grasshoppers and bees.*

What attitude to take? or, as he says, what comfort? On this point the poem wavers inconclusively between philosophical resignation, *apatheia* of the Stoics, 'ghostly solitude,' and the desperate, half-rejoicing cynicism of the epigram already quoted, and of this that comes just before it:

> *O but we dreamed to mend*
> *Whatever mischief seemed*
> *To afflict mankind, but now*
> *That winds of winter blow*
> *Learn that we were crack-pated when we dreamed.*

In part V, the song beginning 'Come let us mock at the great,' the cynicism turns also upon itself at last, for after destroying the pretensions of great, wise and good, he ends:

> *Mock mockers after that*
> *That would not lift a hand maybe*
> *To help good, wise or great*
> *To bar that foul storm out, for we*
> *Traffic in mockery.*

And the poem finishes with an image of chaos come again, evil gathering head, the supposedly banished demonic spirit returning upon the world.

Henceforth Yeats's poetic life is lived in a tension between turning away to 'ghostly solitude,' to 'the cold snows of a dream,' and passionate, brutal, savage, sexual acceptance of 'mire and blood.' In a late poem, 'Meru,' he puts one aspect of the doubleness this way:

> Civilization is hooped together, brought
> Under a rule, under the semblance of peace
> By manifold illusion; but man's life is thought,
> And he, despite his terror, cannot cease
> Ravening through century after century,
> Ravening, raging, and uprooting that he may come
> Into the desolation of reality.

'Man's life is thought.' And it is thought, then, that will lead to 'the desolation of reality.' It reflects upon Locke, in the swoon of whose thought the Garden died. And thought comes whence: from God? from nothing, from the 'dark night' where lay the crowns of Nineveh? I take those crowns to be the towers of the city, and this is certainly the most speculative leap I have to convince you of, but here is the evidence for it, that thought, crown, and tower are explicitly associated by the poet in a phrase drawn from Shelley, who called towers 'thought's crowned powers.' If you can accept the connection on so slender evidence, here are some of the things that follow.

The tower with its winding stair and ruined top is probably Yeats's most deeply inwoven emblem. It is associated on the one hand with ghostly solitude and hermetic meditations such as those of Il Penseroso's Platonist, but also with the opposite, with history, the history of thought in particular, and with involvement in that history. The top of it is sometimes thought of as the human head. The tower is the human counterpart of mountain (such as Meru) or tree, but the tree, the great-rooted blossomer who is neither the leaf the blossom nor the bole but continuously present in all, stands for an inseparable wholeness, of which the tower is the maimed imitation in mind and in history:

> Is every modern nation like the tower,
> Half dead at the top?

The source of that last phrase related tree, tower and mind; it is something Swift said to Edward Young about his apprehensions of approaching madness; pointing at a lightning-blasted oak, 'I shall be like that tree. I shall die first at the top.'

The tower, the top of the tower, is a place of vision, on the lines of Donne's 'Up into the watch-towre get, / And see all things despoil'd of fallacies.' But it is also a wounded, imperfect and ruining vision that is obtainable from there, it is half-dead at the top; and, in 'A Dialogue of Self and Soul,' as well as in 'Blood and the Moon' immediately following, it is a question whether one ought to use its eminence for thinking about history and the chain of past and future, or for denying thought entirely in favor of a darkness indistinguishable from the soul, whether to belong to power or to wisdom:

> *For wisdom is the property of the dead,*
> *A something incompatible with life; and power,*
> *Like everything that has the stain of blood,*
> *A property of the living.*

So far, our associations have moved outward, have diverged from the fable of Locke and the spinning-jenny. And I am conscious of imposing a little on your good nature in getting from the 'Fragments' to the tower on so slim an association as the *crowns* of Nineveh coupled with their association in the poet's mind with towers and with thought on the basis of a phrase taken from Shelley. Now, however, having gone so far away, I may be able to bring us back.

For there is one more main thing about the tower: it contains a winding stair, and this stair develops great density of meaning throughout Yeats's poetry, from the literal 'climb up the narrow winding stairs to bed' of a relatively early poem to 'I declare this tower is my symbol; I declare / This winding, gyring, spiring treadmill of a stair is my ancestral stair,' of 'Blood and the Moon.'

Now this stair, and especially the winding and spiring of it, is preeminently the poet's image for several things: for thought, for the course of history, for the course of the individual's life, for the period after death that he calls 'the dreaming back,' when the soul 'unpacks the loaded pern,' for the spinning motion of the sages in 'Sailing to Byzantium' who are asked to 'perne in a gyre, / And be the singing-masters of my soul,' for the spiral flight of the falcon 'Turning and turning in the widening gyre,' and even for the winding spiral in which the mummy-cloth is wound upon the corpse, which is itself a figure for the life of thought,

> *Wound in mind's pondering,*
> *As mummies in the mummy-cloth are wound.*
>
> ('All Souls' Night')

As one commentator says, bobbin, mummycloth, winding path, and gyre are correlative symbols in Yeats's poetry (Morton Irving Seiden, *William Butler Yeats, The Poet as a Mythmaker* [East Lansing: Michigan State University Press, 1938], p. 263n). To them we may add 'pern' and the poet's note about it telling us that in his childhood the pern was another name for the spool on which thread was wound in the mill near his grandfather's house.

By these considerations we can see a little why the spinning-jenny comes so pat in the small creation story. It is not only a spinning-jenny, but the whirling, spiraling course that is followed not only by the individual's life and in reverse after his death, and at all times by his thought, but also by history, which proceeds in the same spiraling way, a gyre interpenetrated with another that in time will reverse it and spin up its own thread while unspinning the other.

A couple of other items, if you can tolerate more of these strange associative procedures—but if a poet has a logic it may well be an associative one, and hidden to the other kind—may be put into this cluster of thoughts that began with Locke and the spinning-jenny.

As I interpreted that poem, it represents the thought of Locke sinking into the kind of swoon that Blake had called Single Vision and Newton's Sleep. Blake associated Locke with Newton in this single vision which, to him, produced the world as mechanism, from the starry wheels of Urizen's astronomical heavens down to factory and mill; and Yeats tells the same story. The spinning-jenny, among so many other things, is the product of a peculiar kind of vision.

Now vision is not mentioned in those four lines, though they are themselves a vision. But it is everywhere in Yeats's poems, he called his principal expository work on history *A Vision,* and it is filled with notions relating historical tendency to eyesight, and especially to the eyes of statuary. For instance, a brief instance,

When I think of Rome I see always those heads with their world-considering eyes, and those bodies as conventional as the metaphors in a leading article, and compare in my imagination vague Grecian eyes gazing at nothing, Byzantine eyes of drilled ivory staring upon a vision, and those eyelids of China and India, those veiled or half-veiled eyes weary of world and vision alike.

> (*A Vision* [B] [New York: Mac-
> millan, 1938], p. 277)

A few pages later he speaks of a Byzantine technique of drilling the pupil of the eye in ivory, which gives 'to Saint and Angel a look of some great bird staring at miracle.' Birds, it needs no stressing, are this poet's image for the soul: swan, falcon, even 'a portly green-pated bird.'

There is a place, a single line though repeated as a refrain, where ever so much of this constatation of figurative thought—which I have somewhat too laboriously tried to ravel out for its better visibility—occurs in unity. If there truly is something one might call 'poetic thought' distinguishable from the other kind, the rational, linear kind (though existing neither in opposition to it nor in independence of it), this instance is one of its most striking appearances. In 'Meditations in Time of Civil War,' a poem concerned with the same themes as 'Nineteen Hundred and Nineteen,' the sixth part is a lyric called 'The Stare's Nest by My Window.' 'In the West of Ireland,' the poet tells us, 'we call a starling a stare, and during the civil war one built in a hole in the masonry of my bedroom window.' Given that chance—that a starling is called a stare—this is what he makes of it.

> *The bees build in the crevices*
> *Of loosening masonry, and there*
> *The mother birds bring grubs and flies.*
> *My wall is loosening; honey-bees,*
> *Come build in the empty house of the stare.*
>
> *We are closed in, and the key is turned*
> *On our uncertainty; somewhere*
> *A man is killed, or a house burned,*
> *Yet no clear fact to be discerned:*
> *Come build in the empty house of the stare.*
>
> *A barricade of stone or of wood;*
> *Some fourteen days of civil war;*

> *Last night they trundled down the road*
> *That dead young soldier in his blood:*
> *Come build in the empty house of the stare.*
>
> *We had fed the heart on fantasies,*
> *The heart's grown brutal from the fare;*
> *More substance in our enmities*
> *Than in our love; O honey-bees,*
> *Come build in the empty house of the stare.*

The poem is immediately lovely, immediately appealing, all by itself; even more so with our entertaining remote and perhaps parodied echoes from the parable of the lion and the honeycomb. But taken as the flowering of an entire poetic language, for which I have tried to trace through the poetry some of the elements, it becomes even further charged, as the refrain brings indissolubly together in one phrase the meanings I have indicated in separation. The empty house of the stare, for the bird has flown. The empty house of the stair, the winding stair which brings one out to the summit of mind and the end of history, where the tower—we are told by Jeffares that it had never been roofed according to Lutyens's plan but had a concrete roof instead (A. Norman Jeffares, *A Commentary on the Collected Poems of W. B. Yeats,* p. 325)— resembles every modern nation in being 'half-dead at the top.' And the empty house of the stare, the eyes staring out of an empty head, madness within staring at civil war without.

After being so long away, I ought to remind you that the two questions that started me off were: What does the myth about Locke in the Garden tell me about the emergence of the modern world? and Do I believe it? The two might be condensed: What would I be believing if I believed this?

I should be believing first, I suppose, in a world in which imagination, or vision, or mind, is prepotent; but also in a mind so ignorant of its own power that it thought certain thoughts—which indeed it could not help thinking—that turned out to be productive and extremely dangerous in their effect upon the material world, the transformation of which in turn had dangerous, disturbing, perhaps fatally damaging effects upon the mind that had produced the transformation in the first place. This mind, I should have to believe, closed itself down until it saw only a little bit of reality, though it saw that little bit with immensely improved vision and power. As Blake said of this situation,

If the Perceptive Organs close, their objects seem to close also.

(Jerusalem, 34)

But a little bit of reality, no matter how clearly seen, is not reality but fantasy:

We had fed the heart on fantasies,
The heart's grown brutal from the fare. . . .

When I look around me at the world, I think, Yes, I mostly do believe something rather like all that. I have read things rather like it from a good many of the learned and, as I think, the wise; and though they tell the story in a good many different ways, and in terms that differ from the terms others use, each coming at the subject from his own special field of study, they do seem to agree on something that one of them, Erich Heller, put very shrewdly *(The Disinherited Mind* [New York: Meridian Books, 1959]), as from a teacher to students:

Be careful how you interpret the world. It *is* like that.

III. *What Will Suffice*

In the second lecture, on the basis of one small example, I approached the question of what belief has to do with poetry. And I have an obscure sense of having touched on something of great importance to modern poets and their readers; of such great importance that I feel bound to attempt its further elucidation though aware of my probable inadequacy for the job.

It seems to me that my labors of interpretation in that lecture permit the following general inferences. A poem exists in itself, in the sense that you can read it and as they say *understand it* alone. But it exists in a very different way for the reader who also knows the poet's other works; and in a still different way for the reader who attempts to apply it to the world, the language, history, tradition, whence it arose and to which in some unsettled sense it always belongs.

All these statements modify one another; none can stand all by itself. Even to read the Yeats epigram all by itself, for instance, it helps to know even if only a little the traditional world on which it draws, for noun after noun—Locke, the Garden, God, the spinning-jenny— requires more of the reader than that he be that average user of the language posited by certain schools of philosophy; this average user of the language is a figment, and he could not read a poem of this sort even if he existed.

So a single poem is to some extent interpretable by itself, though it may require of the interpreter some bits of knowledge not simply lexical but historical or traditional or whatever. But it exists also as a focus for the contemplation of two worlds outside itself. One is the world of the poet's work entire, with such manifold and strange interrelations as I spent last lecture trying to trace for Yeats—a world in which objects so far apart in ordinary speech as a spinning-jenny and a tower may share the same meanings. The other is the world we believe we live in. That world, its mode of existence, is also an object of our belief as much as of our knowledge, or more. It is of poetry in relation to that world that I shall try to speak this time. Much to your relief, I shall leave Yeats, Locke, and the spinning-jenny, and base upon other examples.

All my examples here have to do with what I called The Great Change, and they all, whether overtly or obliquely, have something to do with science. So I shall feel better for repeating my caution. I am not against science as a perfectly, or maybe better an imperfectly, proper activity for human beings to pursue; and I don't think the poets from whom I draw my illustrations are either. But poetry, I say again, exists to consider the wholeness of things as far as human beings using language can do so. That may not be very far. But it seems essential to stress that these poems, like the Yeats one, are myths of creation and fall; they seek to say, to give a shape to, some very great something that has happened in the world; and in this attempt they do not see science as an isolable pursuit at all, any more than they would see as isolable pursuits business, education, revolution, nationalism, racism, or any other of the manifold of fictitious entities whose perfectly real results characterize the present age. It is the manifold itself that they are trying to see as a unity; consequently their language may be sometimes riddling, and is almost always very abstract. That is something about them much against the tendency of the age, of which I have said enough already perhaps, to stress immediate sense experience as the highest value.

One more introductory remark. My examples range from neutral to apocalyptic in tone. That may be a matter of my own dour and gloomy nature or it may not. But I should say that there were poets, and there may still be some, who in their poems view The Great Change as a matter for difficult rejoicings. Whitman seems to have thought that such things as the opening of the Suez Canal and the laying of the Atlantic cable were, or represented, or foreshadowed 'the venturing of the soul into the seas of God'; Crane supposed a good deal more desperately that his bridge might of its curveship lend a myth to God; with these I am not concerned.

Wallace Stevens, who gave it as one of his three requirements for a supreme fiction, meaning probably an epic poem, or a poem which should unify the meanings of a complex age as epics did for what seem simpler ages, that It Must Be Abstract, wrote a kind of programmatic outline of The Great Change and its meaning for poetry; it is called 'Of Modern Poetry,' and it begins:

> The poem of the mind in the act of finding
> What will suffice. It has not always had
> To find: the scene was set; it repeated what
> Was in the script.
> > Then the theatre was changed
> To something else. Its past was a souvenir.

This needs, I think, no interpreting; nor shall I quote the whole of it, but only a single striking phrase of definition that I had not noticed before this time of reading. 'The mind in the act' becomes the metaphor for the whole process, it is taken literally that the mind is an actor in an improvisation; and he says presently that the actor is 'a metaphysician in the dark.' There is so much in that phrase that I am unwilling to comment on it at all; it either is or it ain't: a metaphysician in the dark, an actor who is a metaphysician in the dark. . . . Poetry, it is worth observing, is a place where you find remarks of that sort. And I am willing to accept the reverse relation: wherever you find remarks of that sort, you are in the presence of poetry. Scientists, for instance, make such wonderful sayings quite often, though sometimes you have to winkle 'em out of great chunks of surrounding stuff.

Schrödinger, in his book *What Is Life?* (New York: Macmillan, 1946) juxtaposes two sayings, one by Eddington and one by Sherrington:

1. The frank realization that physical science is concerned with a world of shadows is one of the most significant of recent advances.
2. Mind, for anything perception can compass, goes therefore in our spatial world more ghostly than a ghost.

Whence we are permitted to put together 'a world of shadows wondered at by ghosts.' Schrödinger himself is just as good when he speaks of the entire course of the world before the brain existed as 'a play before empty seats.' Such things not only approach the quality of, but also have great bearing on, the mind as an actor who is a metaphysician in the dark.

Stevens is not only programmatic, but to this limited extent optimistic: he views the mind as actively responding to the changed conditions. My other authors are less concerned with what is to be done than with representing the change itself in its magnitude, its decisiveness, and the horror or despair the contemplation of it is able to produce. Here are two balanced sentence-stanzas by W. H. Auden, somewhat coyly entitled 'In Father's Footsteps.'

> *Our hunting fathers told the story*
> *Of the sadness of the creatures,*
> *Pitied the limits and the lack*
> *Set in their finished features;*
> *Saw in the lion's intolerant look,*
> *Behind the quarry's dying glare,*
> *Love raging for the personal glory*
> *That reason's gift would add,*
> *The liberal appetitie and power,*
> *The rightness of a god.*
>
> *Who, nurtured in that fine tradition,*
> *Predicted the result,*
> *Guessed love by nature suited to*
> *The intricate ways of guilt,*
> *That human ligaments could so*
> *His southern gestures modify*

And make it his mature ambition
To think no thought but ours,
To hunger, work illegally,
And be anonymous?

> (*The Collected Poems of W. H.*
> *Auden* [New York: Random
> House, 1976])

The poem is far from clear to me in the historical placement of its first term: the hunting fathers might belong to the British Indian Army or to prehistoric times. But I think that makes not much difference to the sense of this whole movement from confidence to gloom, from forceful assertion to plaintive question. From totemistic identification and animistic readings-in, from pathetic fallacy—powerful so far as it is pathetic, said Ruskin, and feeble so far as it is fallacious—we progress in the second stanza to the image of Love as a displaced and stateless person. The whole poem, so beautifully turned and so abstract it might have a large number of applications, seems to balance on some such twinned proposition as this: in the very course of confidently reasoning human significance into the creation, men somehow exiled human significance from the creation, and with it themselves. The hunting fathers were either mistaken about the presence of Love behind the quarry's dying glare, or they were mistaken about Love's nature. In any event, what happened turned out catastrophic; no one nurtured in that fine tradition, possibly the tradition of enlightened self-interest which Dostoevsky excoriates as enlightened greed, could have known how the enterprise was going to turn out, as Love progressed from beast to proletariat without, so far as Auden is concerned in this poem, any noticeable or noteworthy interval among uncoerced human beings.

Here is a poem by Louis Simpson called 'The Riders Held Back' (*Selected Poems* [New York: Harcourt, Brace & World, 1965]). Or at least here is part of it, for like one or two other of my illustrations it is too long to quote; which matters a little less than it might, for the middle is too full of cute poetry writing anyhow; yet I think the whole survives it. This time the story of The Great Change is told with particular stress on art and intellect, and it is dated to the Renaissance. The riders of the title, who might be medieval knights, come upon Botticelli's Graces in a glade, dancing. Why do they dance? 'Said one, "It is an intellectual joy, / The Renaissance."' And she goes on expounding the wonders of this intellectual joy, with a couple of sinister reservations and forebodings: 'It is the music of astronomy, not men, we love,' and the news that while Raphael and Petrarch belong to the place. 'Michael is not here, who carved the brute / Unfinished men.'

Their dance inspires in the hypnotized riders a vision of 'Towers and ramparts glittering with lights, / Like Paradise.' But when they awaken the dancers are gone, a distant trumpet sounding, with this result:

> *We galloped to it. In the forest then*
> *Banners and shields*
> *Were strewn like leaves; and there were many slain*
> *In the dark fields.*

So in a few stanzas we are taken from the vision of *Primavera* to something more like that of the *Rout of San Romano,* the same picture that inspired a neglected master, Ben Belitt, to his wonderful poem 'Battle-Piece,' which I should much like to deal with here save that it is too long and perhaps too intricate as well for a lecture.

Richard Wilbur has a beautiful poem called 'Merlin Enthralled,' in which he views what I am calling The Great Change by means of legend. Again, the poem is too long to quote entire, and I must summarize with the help of phrases here and there. The story tells how, when Merlin was seduced and locked away by Niniane, something went out of the enterprise of the round table, and out of the world, too. Arthur and Gawen go out riding, aimlessly riding, the poem says:

> *Merlin, Merlin, their hearts cried, where are you hiding?*
> *In all the world was no unnatural sound.*
>
> *Mystery watched them riding glade by glade;*
> *They saw it darkle from under leafy brows;*
> *But leaves were all its voice, and squirrels made*
> *An alien fracas in the ancient boughs.*
>
> *Once by a lake-edge something made them stop.*
> *Yet what they found was the thumping of a frog,*
> *Bugs skating on the shut water-top,*
> *Some hairlike algae bleaching on a log.*

There follows a middle section dealing with Merlin's sleep and his forgetfulness of Arthur and the Court:

Slowly the shapes of searching men and horses
Escaped him as he dreamt on that high bed:
History died. . . .

And as he ceased from dreaming into deeper and simple sleep, we are to understand, a certain great reality departed from the world because he no longer had the world in mind. The poem ends with Arthur's being made aware that this is so, though not of why it is so:

Fate would be fated; dreams desire to sleep.
This the forsaken will not understand.
Arthur upon the road began to weep
And said to Gawen Remember when this hand

Once haled a sword from stone; now no less strong
It cannot dream of such a thing to do.
Their mail grew quainter as they clopped along.
The sky became a still and woven blue.

> (in *Things of This World* [New
> York: Harcourt Brace & Com-
> pany, 1956])

It is hard for me to discuss this poem with you, though I shall have to try. Apart from the tact, skill, and modest assurance with which it is written—all qualities very easily and often disparaged these days in favor of various unbuttoned alternatives—it makes a strong and personal appeal to me. I think I experience this appeal whenever—and it isn't so often—a modern poet returns to legendary figures and themes not for decoration but in order that we shall see deeply into their present truth. When this happens, when, as here, the poet has heard the very footsteps of Astraea leaving the earth, I feel that literary criticism is scarcely to the point, and I answer with love and sorrow to his thought, as well as with that impersonal gladness, that elation, that comes when beautiful and accurate saying seems to overcome the sorrow of what is said. I do not believe it is the lecturer's office to persuade his hearers of the beauty of something he thinks beautiful; it gets him into all sorts of ridiculous postures; but I couldn't resist saying that much.

How is this poem about what I am calling The Great Change? It is timeless and mythological rather than historical. Perhaps, for me, that is one of its many excellences, that by its legendary setting it tells me that The Great Change is not historical only, but primarily metaphysical and psychological; something we have a certain experience of under today's historical conditions, and yesterday's, but also something we should have experienced, though in other terms perhaps, whenever and wherever we lived; a change that can become historical, in fact, only because it is first the experience of every individual at all times.

Merlin is a remote and deep and powerful figure. As far as I know no one, not Malory certainly and not even T. H. White, has truly told the story as Merlin saw it, though maybe before making so round a statement I should go back and read again Tennyson's attempt, and Robinson's. He is a magician, whose magic is for the most part not identifiably of any practical use to people; his capture by Niniane, or Nimue, or Vivien, is also a most mysterious business, for it suggests his magic is mediate, it brings to the earth powers derived elsewhere and subordinated to someone else. In Wilbur's poem the magic that Merlin did is seen to be imagination, relating to will, to dream, to spirit, with their incredible power of overcoming the visible and natural world as it were by poetizing it full of spirits. When Merlin fades from the world, the supernatural entities fade also, leaving bewilderment behind. For these supernatural entities may be easily enough derided and mocked into nonexistence by the skeptical under their traditional names, such names as Jehovah, Lucifer, Michael, Ahriman, and so on; but at some peril to all of us, for if those names are fictitious names, and they are, they nevertheless name perfectly real forces able to produce perfectly real and spectacular results in what we call the real world. The names presently given to such beings—mind, spirit, will, soul, imagination, intellectual light—are also under the attack of a skeptical reasoning power minded to daylight alone and entire; and like the giant forms of mythology and legend these too are being driven out of poetry—for most poets shamefacedly acquiesce in the skepticism around them, careless or unaware that they are acquiescing in the destruction of their art and their vocation together. But here, says Gerard Manley Hopkins, 'the faithful waver, the faithless fable and miss.' And Shakespeare in a wonderful passage shows us again that this question is not a question simply for our own day alone, but for always:

> *They say miracles are past; and we have our*
> *philosophical persons, to make modern and*
> *familiar, things supernatural and causeless.*

Hence it is that we make trifles of terrors,
ensconcing ourselves into seeming knowledge,
when we should submit ourselves to an unknown fear.

(Lafeu, *All's Well* Act II Scene 3,
ll. 1–6)

Erich Heller (*The Disinherited Mind* [New York: Meridian Books, 1959], p. 205), applying that passage to the writings of Franz Kafka, adds that 'our age has witnessed the abdication of the philosophical persons.' I think I see what he means. But it just doesn't seem to be so, though it ought to be. Devils and angels together, goblins and nymphs alike, appear to be progressively forbidden the poets just as they have progressively been exiled from the world, in the interest, it is supposed, of evidence, reason, clear thinking, common sense; but I rather doubt the poets are in a better position for that; and the last state of them is like enough to be worse than the first. For poetry was once the place where these entities did their proper work, where the exact degree of their fictitiousness could be measured against the exact degree of their quite real powers, and both could be experienced ideally, not fatally in the world of action. As Rudolf Steiner said so shrewdly, Think these thoughts without believing them. Which is like what Keats said about the poetical character taking no harm from either the dark or the bright side of things—because, he said, they both end in speculation. In that sense, poetry would be the good place for experiencing mankind's brightest and his darkest mythological fantasies— poetry, and not the newspapers, the Congress, and so on. As Blake said in the Preface to *Jerusalem,* 'We who live on earth can do nothing of ourselves, everything is done by spirits' . . . and just as we are about to say brightly, Aw, come off it, Willy, there ain't no spirits, he adds: 'No less than digestion or sleep.'

The great difficulty or impossibility—the hazard, as Heller calls it—for modern poetry has been in attaining to a view of the universe which shall be equally and simultaneously real and transpicuous, physical and mental, and to do this—here is the tightrope part of the act—without on the one hand becoming a religion fully outfitted with priesthood and theology (or criticism), and without, on the other hand, pretending that science either doesn't exist or doesn't matter. I do not think, myself, that our resolutions of this difficulty have been triumphant ones; indeed, it is perhaps a built-in feature of 'the modern' in poetry to couple ever more extravagant and hysterical claims to save the world with the actual products—those little poems, remember?—that appear as ever more marginal and incapable of saving even themselves.

So perhaps what I am responding so deeply to in Wilbur's poem about Merlin is his steadfast and poignant acknowledgment of what magic, and what poetry, are about. It is part of the pathos, maybe, that this acknowledgment can be made precisely and only because magic, and poetry, have gone out of the world; just as Freud said that certain thoughts can be admitted to consciousness only under pain of being denied. It is not that Arthur is older, his hand less strong to hale a sword from stone; but now 'it cannot *dream* of such a thing to do.' And those quiet concluding lines:

> *Their mail grew quainter as they clopped along.*
> *The sky became a still and woven blue.*

I like to think, though I've never asked the poet about it, that their decisive effect on me is produced by a particular association; that is, to those movies we used to see in childhood, where the camera at the beginning shows us the naive and storybook illustration, whence gradually emerge the real persons, who however at the end are absorbed back into such an illustration, becoming, ever so quietly and finally, storybook persons again. Arthur and Gawen have become obsolete to life, their mail grew quainter as they clopped along—'clopped' especially makes them out a bit toylike and diminutive—but they also, with an effect at once sorrowful and consoling—as the grownups used to say to us, whispering and holding hands, 'Don't worry, dear, it's only a movie'—they also merge seamlessly into the ground, the work of art, the story.

If I introduce here a small poem of my own, I should do so without apology. It is part of the theme, one more variation on the sense of a Great Change. Besides, it will produce a probably welcome change of tone.

IDEA

> *Idea blazes in darkness, a lonely star.*
> *The witching hour is not twelve, but one.*
> *Pure thought, in principle, some say, is near*
> *Madness, but the independent mind thinks on,*
> *Breathing and burning, abstract as the air.*

Supposing all this were a game of chess.
One learned to do without the pieces first,
And then the board; and finally, I guess,
Without the game. The lightship gone adrift,
Endangering others with its own distress.

O holy light! All other stars are gone,
The shapeless constellations sag and fall
Till navigation fails, though ships go on
This merry, mad adventure as before
Their single-minded masters meant to drown.

Some friends have found that a bit riddling. I find it so myself. But I introduced it here not in order that I should give explanations; rather to identify one thought in it that seems pertinent to the theme, and that I have not much seen discussed. That thought is itself about a striking characteristic of thought, that it begins by separating things that are first found inextricably one, and then spends years of arduous work trying to put them back together. The thought comes up in stanza two, in relation to the game of chess, and its parody of our ways of thinking, especially our ways of thinking about the beginnings of things, may be clearer if I reverse the process outlined in the poem and ask: if you are inventing the game of chess, which do you invent first, the pieces or the board? Another version would be: which came first, piano sonatas or pianos? And another: The architects built New York City; there it was, under the sun, immense. And one said: What d'you think would happen, now, if we introduced people into this situation? Perhaps, even probably, I am wrong; or even if I am right we may have no workable alternative; but I do have the strong impression that the artifice called thought, and behind it the second nature called language, have built into them this strange and powerful discontinuous way of dealing with continuous things.

For the rest, I suppose, the poem qualifies as pertinent to the theme of The Great Change because it represents intellect trying to go it alone. But I spare you my commentary, and go on to one last example.

THE EMANCIPATORS

When you ground the lenses and the moons swam free
From that great wanderer; when the apple shone
Like a sea-shell through your prism, voyager;

When, dancing in pure flame, the Roman mercy,
Your doctrines blew like ashes from your bones;

Did you think, for an instant, past the numerals
Jellied in Latin like bacteria in broth,
Snatched for by holy Europe like a sign?
Past sombre tables inched out with the lives
Forgotten or clapped for by the wigged Societies?

You guessed this? The earth's face altering with iron,
The smoke ranged like a wall against the day?
—The equations metamorphose into use: the free
Drag their slight bones from tenements to vote
To die with their children in your factories.

Man is born in chains, and everywhere we see him dead.
On your earth they sell nothing but our lives.
You knew that what you died for was our deaths?
You learned, those years, that what men wish is Trade?
It was you who understood; it is we who change.

This is a sweeping indictment indeed, at least to a first look, though a second will show it as tragic, and under the sway of fatal necessity. Perhaps I should balance it out with a similar indictment from the other side, this time in prose. Some years ago I heard a Nobel Laureate (as they are called) in physics address a few hundred people: 'We physicists were not responsible for the atom bomb,' he said, and then, leaning forward: 'You want to know who was responsible for the atom bomb? I will tell you who was responsible.' And in a voice of thunder or as near as he could come to that, '*You* were responsible for the atom bomb!'

Returning to poetry, the people addressed in the first stanza and thereafter are Galileo and Newton and Giordano Bruno. I was informed of this in a note by the poet, and rather regretted that, for by some remarkable chance I had figured it out for myself.

Galileo was the first to apply the telescope to astronomical uses, and the moons he saw swim free were those of Jupiter and Saturn. Newton comes in more complicatedly; the apple for gravitation, of course, the prism for his work in optics, with a reminiscence of Wordsworth's lines in *The Prelude* about the statue at Cambridge:

Of Newton with his prism and silent face,
The marble index of a mind for ever
Voyaging through strange seas of Thought, alone.

(III, 61–63)

The sea-shell, I suspect without being able to prove, comes from a crossing of two thoughts: one, of Newton's own, makes a curious contrast with Wordsworth's 'seas of Thought,' for in it Newton compares himself to a little boy wandering on the shores of the illimitable ocean of Truth and occasionally picking up a pebble which delighted him; a pebble, not a sea-shell. The sea-shell may have entered by way of *The Prelude* also, where in the great apocalyptic dream of Book Five—another story of The Great Change, by the way—stone and shell become the emblems of geometric truth and poetry respectively.

Bruno was burned at Rome (the Roman mercy) in 1600 for being a premature Copernican and drawing philosophical consequences from astronomical grounds.

The theory of the poem, then, is that these saints and martyrs of the scientific vision released apocalyptic powers upon the world. They are, with a kind of ludicrous pathos, responsible and not responsible for what happened; and it is remarkable how our examples have recurred to this point: How could we know? and at the same time How could we have failed to know? Thus Yeats of his Athenians: 'None dared admit, if such a thought were his . . . ' and Auden: 'Who, nurtured in that fine tradition, predicted the result?' And so here: Did you think . . . ? You guessed . . . ? You knew . . . ? More directly than the others, this poet speaks direly of and for the wholeness of life: admitting the triumphs of science and technology, are they separable from the disasters of science and technology? In a bitter and picturesque metaphor he sees the mathematical language invading the holy language, forerunning disease: 'the numerals / Jellied in Latin like bacteria in broth.' And savagely he reduces Rousseau's initial proposition in *The Social Contract* to 'Man is born in chains, and everywhere we see him dead.' The point of the argument is that science, even mathematics however pure, does not come alone: the equations metamorphose into use, they enter into politics and trade; the *libido sciendi* cannot hold itself free and aloof from the immense changes it will produce in the practical world where people are born and where they die; or, in the pathetic and terrible last line, it can, it does:

It was you who understood; it is we who change.

Closely attended to, this poem is not an assault upon science. It represents a tragical history, and represents it tragically, that is to say, helplessly, with woe and wonder:

You knew that what you died for was our deaths?

This poem was written by the late Randall Jarrell, and it will be appropriate for me to make of him the chief illustration of my closing remarks.

Jarrell and I were enough of an age, enough of a critical temper of mind, enough of the same literary community, that we reviewed one another's slender volumes one after another, maybe as many as three times each. We were upon the whole respectful, friendly, even now and then admiring, but we were also nothing if not critical; the burden of my criticism was that Jarrell often wrote slovenly; and of his, that I tried to be funny in serious places.

Now, four years after Randall Jarrell died, his publishers have sent me *The Complete Poems* (New York: Farrar, Straus & Giroux, 1968). And I look at it with at first a naive and then a deepening wonder. Why, it's as fat as the *Collected Wallace Stevens,* I say, hefting it in my hand. It's got more pages than the *Collected Yeats.* So this is what came of those slender volumes year by year!

About the greatness of Randall Jarrell's poetry I am not ready to speak, save to say that he makes a fair candidate for the adjective, not so much because he wrote a few beautiful poems, but more because, as one could not have seen so well before *The Complete Poems,* his poems fit with one another, lead on from one to another, reinforce one another's meanings, in such a way as to suggest a coherent and articulated world of their own, in just the way that Stevens's poems do, and Yeats's poems do. This is heartening for more than one reason. It is heartening because it shows that the beautiful is still among possible things. It is heartening especially to see that during a period when literary people were howling in the usual way, on one side about how poetry was dead, on the other side about how new techniques and modern idioms were going to transform the world, a real poet was patiently going about his business of using the language in recognizably the same way that poets had used the language since Chaucer's time, and gradually deepening the articulations of a vision uniquely his own.

Jarrell is peculiarly appropriate for the ending of this essay about The Great Change, although I didn't know that when I started to write, for he is preeminently the poet of that change. The word 'change' itself is one he made poignantly his; it echoes from poem to poem, and often forms the climax and conclusion and lesson. From his use of it I am able to see more clearly what I meant, or what I should have meant, in speaking of this Great Change.

I at first identified it, in connection with Yeats, with the First World War, though even at first I allowed the War to be a peculiarly dramatic and apocalyptic revelation of it, and not it itself. But as I studied my examples, I was led on to say that quite apart from any historical attachment The Great Change existed always and in every individual's life; in effect it is only for that reason, of a metaphysical and psychological priority, that the Great Change can get into history at all. Also, though for the present age science and technology appear as the great agents of that change, I am persuaded that before science and technology were, at least in anything like their modern forms, The Great Change was. Perhaps after all it is nothing but growing up, a peculiar form of growing up, or else the sudden after-realization of what growing up has entailed. Jarrell sees it particularly in respect to children who suddenly penetrate behind the storybooks, the fairy tales, and see death in its lonesomeness, its decisive and destructive effect on all that is loved, especially the self. In two examples, both of them about children in a library, he seems to think the two opposites that form one only thought; at the end of one, speaking to the books on the shelves, he says:

> We learned from you so much about so many things
> But never what we were; and yet you made us that.
> We found in you the knowledge for a life
> But not the will to use it in our lives
> That were always, somehow, so different from the books'.
> We learn from you to understand, but not to change.

> (*The Complete Poems*, p. 99)

And at the end of the other, 'In slow perambulation up and down the shelves / Of the universe,' the children are 'seeking . . . who knows except themselves?'

What some escape to, some escape: if we find Swann's
Way better than our own, and trudge on at the back
Of the north wind to—to—somewhere east
Of the sun, west of the moon, it is because we live

By trading another's sorrow for our own; another's
Impossibilities, still unbelieved in, for our own . . .
'I am myself still'? For a little while, forget:
The world's selves cure that short disease, myself,
And we see bending to us, dewy-eyed, the great
CHANGE, dear to all things not to themselves endeared.

(*The Complete Poems*, pp. 106–107)

That is one side of it. Perhaps the other is the hope against hope, the hope beyond hope, of the Woman in the Washington Zoo, saying so simply and appallingly to the vulture whom she sees as man disguised and wild brother:

You know what I was,
You see what I am: change me, change me!

The poem of the mind in the act of finding what will suffice. . . . That is where I started, with Stevens's patient, questioning, explorative efforts of definition. How better close than with the answering voice of William Yeats, answering to one troubled time from another troubled time?

I turn away and shut the door, and on the stair
Wonder how many times I could have proved my worth
In something that all others understand or share;
But O! ambitious heart, had such a proof drawn forth
A company of friends, a conscience set at ease,
It had but made us pine the more. The abstract joy,
The half-read wisdom of daemonic images,
Suffice the ageing man as once the growing boy.

('Meditations in Time of Civil War,' VII)

These will suffice, they will endure, they will teach.

has been set on a VIP composing machine by The Composing Room of Michigan, Inc. in a typeface commonly known as Garamond. Named after the famous sixteenth-century French type designer and letter cutter, it is representative of the classic and elegant faces developed by the Parisian punchcutters that gradually displaced the old Venetian designs originating with da Spira and Jenson. Garamond is also the first face which treated the roman and italic as constituents of the same fount. ¶Printed and bound at Halliday Lithograph Corporation, the paper is Warren's 66 Antique, an entirely acid- and groundwood-free sheet.